T0327831

HOUSE MAGIC

HOUSE MAGIC

A HANDBOOK TO MAKING EVERY HOME A SACRED SANCTUARY

AURORA KANE

To my sister, Gaye, whose laughter, beauty, courage, and love are her magic spells.

First published in 2020 by Wellfleet, an imprint of The Quarto Group,
142 West 36th Street, 4th Floor, New York, NY 10018, USA
T (212) 779-4972 F (212) 779-6058 www.Quarto.com

Wellfleet titles are also available at discount for retail, wholesale, promotional, and bulk purchase. For details, contact the Special Sales Manager by email at specialsales@quarto.com or by mail at The Quarto Group, Attn: Special Sales Manager, 100 Cummings Center Suite 265D, Beverly, MA 01915 USA.

10 9 8 7 6 5

ISBN: 978-1-57715-211-8

Library of Congress Control Number: 2020943024

Publisher: Rage Kindelsperger
Managing Editor: Cara Donaldson
Creative Director: Laura Drew
Project Editors: Leeann Moreau and Keyla Pizarro-Hernández
Cover and Interior Design: Laura Klynstra

Printed in China

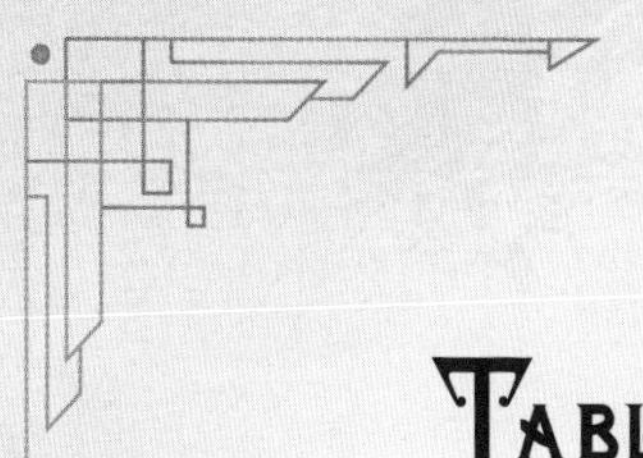
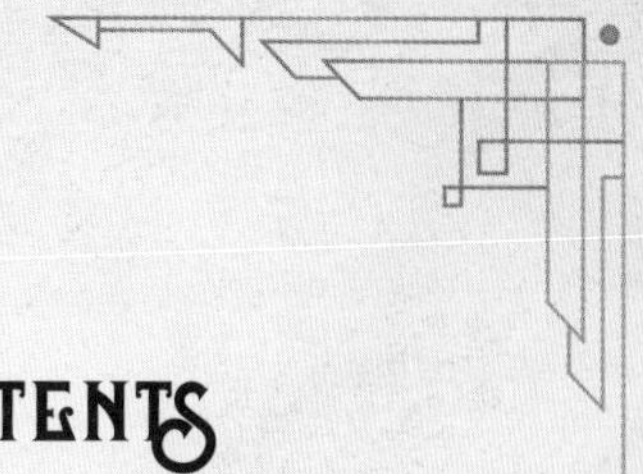

Table of Contents

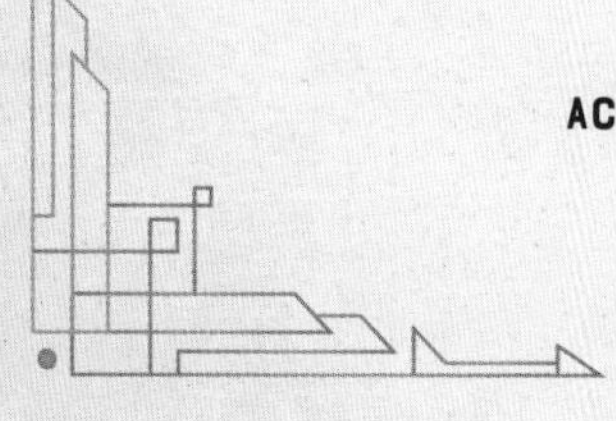

The WELCOME mat is just the start—a hearty fond "hello!"
For here you'll find an inner peace and ways to make it glow.

Reach deep inside, your powers there, though hidden they may be,
Will bloom and grow in ways to know just when to grasp life's lead.

When elements of Earth and Sky join in the merry rite,
As above, so below—stirs enchantment and delight.

So tarry not, for once you find the secret to its spell,
Your house and home, bid "enter all," those here who wish to dwell.

Where love abounds and charms do sweep all evil from its door,
Your heart becomes a wishing well; your home its guiding shore.

INTRODUCTION

Your home. Your palace. Your nest. Your kingdom. Your sanctuary. *Sanctuary*. No matter how you describe your "dwelling," it is, ultimately, your sanctuary. Your place of love and nurture, comfort and safety.

But it is not just a "place." A house has a spirit all its own, derived from the energy of the land it sits on and the vibrations of the natural materials from which it is built. When alone in your house, close your eyes and listen to its heartbeat, hear its message, feel its energy. That innate magic in your house can be used—in combination with your personal energy and magic multiplied by Earth, the sky, and Nature—to live your most joyful, purposeful, healthy, and happy life.

Shaping your home into a sacred sanctuary is closely tied with living in tune with Nature. As we become more in tune with Nature's energies—from the wind, Sun, Moon, and Earth and all her bounty—we can use those vibrational elements to enhance intentions and communicate with the Universe . . . sending out wishes and hopes and dreams that can, ultimately, become our reality.

Working in rhythm with Nature means slowing the pace and savoring the moment. It means looking inward and hearing the present, not worrying about tomorrow or things we cannot control. It gives you the freedom to own the life you want and take responsibility for making it a reality. It is a breather from everyday stress. It is a child's hug, a neighbor's wave, a smile from a stranger, a comfortable bed. It is a sigh of renewal.

Here, we'll consider the spirit of the house as well as the personalities of its rooms and uncover ways to enhance, utilize, discover, and change their magical potential in your life. Tapping into your inner domestic goddess and connecting with the powers of Nature, you'll enhance your own vibrational energies and bring your home in tune with you.

You'll protect your home's inhabitants from evil, banish negative energies, set intentions to transform your life, and simply reflect on all you have to be grateful for. We'll use the power of light, sound, color, scent, crystals, and Nature's flora and fauna to make home even homier, and a place to thrive in whatever ways you wish.

Escape from everyday stress into the magic of your home. Burst forth renewed to take on the world, or at least change it for the better in your own personal way.

MANIFESTING A MAGICAL LIFE

May a life fulfilled be the greatest gift of all.

Though "magic" implies something supernatural, it's really the opposite here. The powers to manifest a magical life and create a magical home are well within you, within the heavens, within Earth, within Nature—and within reach. Living your best magical life and manifesting your most magical dreams start with a few simple ideas:

Be kind to yourself—your magical powers are contained within.

Be kind to others—their magical powers can amplify yours.

Be kind to Earth—her magical powers support everything.

Be a believer.

Think of your magical life as a garden: Take care to prepare the soil (that's you) properly. Carefully sow the seeds of growth (your intentions). Tend to those seeds with water, sunshine, and weeding (that's life). Celebrate your bountiful harvest (achieving goals based on set intentions). Share the wealth (give back) and evaluate which seeds thrived and which may need to be replaced with a different crop (assess and re-tune your goals). And, finally, put the garden to bed for winter (self-care and reflection).

Among the everyday chaos, creating a magical life sounds big, but it is completely doable with a few consistent steps: Take time for yourself—you'll be better for others that way. Start small and be consistent in your actions. Know your intent and your actions will naturally align to manifest the results you desire.

You don't need much to get started—an understanding of intentions and how to set them and the belief in your powers within will get you far—and you can build a tool kit along the way, if you so desire. We'll explore different ideas throughout the book.

Tend to your precious gifts and discover the person you can be within the protective walls of your magical home. And, when you're ready, shake the dust off your magic carpet and let's go for a ride.

SETTING INTENTIONS

To fill your home and life with magic, you must know what you want, imprint it on your soul, and commit to making it happen. We're all busy, so consciously taking time to reflect and set intentions—chart your course, check progress, and rediscover the way when lost—lets us utilize the quiet to hear what our hearts are saying.

As our world gets increasingly noisier and busier, finding time for quiet is necessary to soothe our souls. Shutting out the chaotic clutter is a great first step, but really taking time to be quiet—with no agenda—can promote the creation of new ideas. Schedule quiet time in meditation to uncover what you may not notice in the busyness of the day. As your mind and heart expand, so will your natural intuition. You'll feel what is important and can set your intentions to achieve those priorities you visualize for you and your family—to create your most magical life.

As all things are made of energy, and all energy vibrates at different intensities, so, too, do your intentions. This Universal energy means all things are connected and energies, like ripples in a pond, expand outward and allow the energy to influence results and come back to you many times multiplied.

To begin, define your intentions: What do you want? What do you need? What do you wish for your family? What needs attention in your life? These are good places to start. Reach deep into your soul to acknowledge, without fear, what is important to you.

Defining intentions keeps us focused and living in the present, mindfully, and can help improve our overall well-being. It is also important to live mindfully *without judgment*, learning to accept what is and work for better circumstances, as we desire.

When you wake, take a minute to breathe in and out slowly and purposely. Greet the Sun and be grateful for a new day. Set your intentions for the day:

I will give as much as I receive.
I will make one new connection that can help my job search.
Though times are tough, I offer thanks for what I have.

It's often advised to plan your life and live your plan. This is intention setting in action.

USING COLORS TO SET INTENTIONS

Use colors and their corresponding vibrational energies as you blend your magical home into an intention-filled life. Think **candles, paint, fabric, crystals, flowers, accessories—even food, makeup, and manicures**—to help you establish the foundations of what's important to you and set the mood throughout your home.

It's important to note that colors are frequently assigned different or multiple meanings, so experiment, have fun, and stay in tune with your intuition—use the colors that feel right or speak to you.

BLACK
protection, security

BLUE
calm, healing, health

BRIGHT ORANGE
happiness

BRONZE
experience, prosperity, strength

BROWN

feeling grounded, longevity, nature

DARK BLUE

peace, tranquility

DEEP, BRIGHT PINK

creativity, glamour

GREEN

children, fertility, feeling grounded, friendship, good luck nature, prosperity, wealth

GOLD
elegance, prestige, prosperity, success

LAVENDER
intuition

MUTED ORANGE
warmth

ORANGE
healing, health

PURPLE
success, prosperity, wealth

RED/DEEP RED

passion, protection, romantic love, security

SILVER

modern, moonlight, sophistication

SOFT PINK

calm, friendship, tenderness

WHITE

cleansing, protection, security; white can also stand in for any color you want but don't have; visualize the desired color as you light a white candle and imagine the hue you wish.

YELLOW

communication, creativity, happiness, joy, warmth

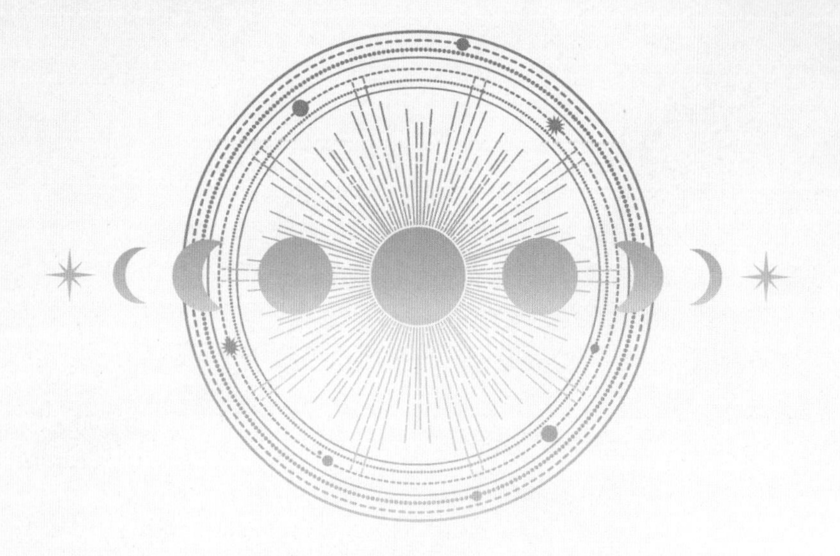

THE MOON'S GUIDING FORCES

Use the waxing (growing) and waning (diminishing) energies of the Moon's changing phases to set, implement, evaluate, and revise, achieve, celebrate, and assess your intention-filled life. Coordinating your thoughts and dreams and plans with the Moon's natural cycle can help you achieve all you hope for—for your family and yourself.

The most typical items placed under the Moon's healing touch are crystals and gemstones for clearing, or resetting, their energy vibrations. However, you can use these same energies to infuse items important to you or critical to your goals with specific intention. Are you an artist? Charge you paints and paintbrushes. Maps for travelers. Pens for writers. Books for students. Water for rehydration or bathing. Salt for cleansing. Coins for abundance and sharing . . . the options are only limited by your imagination and desired intentions.

To start, cleanse new items, or remove any negative energies they may be carrying with them, first before charging or recharging, which is simply resupplying and amplifying their inherent energies. Simply place the items you wish to cleanse in the Moon's light—outdoors, if safe, on a windowsill receiving the Moon's light, or another area open to the Moon.

Consider the Moon's eight phases—which span, roughly, one month from start to finish—and the associated power they can add to your intentions.

Phase 1, New Moon: A new beginning. The New Moon's phase can unlock your intuition and encourage you to take stock of what's needed in your life.

Phase 2, Waxing Crescent: Growing light awakens intentions. The growing energies of this Moon's phase stir activity. Set your intentions and plant their seeds to sprout.

Phase 3, First Quarter Moon: Stronger vibrations sharpen intentions and intuition. Use the Moon's vibrations to magnify your energies toward reaching your goals.

Phase 4, Waxing Gibbous: Increased excitement and energy spur action. In the Moon's growing light, evaluate progress and dispel any shadowy doubt.

Phase 5, Full Moon: Celebrate achievements and feel gratitude for the abundance the earth provides. Use the power of the Full Moon to illuminate your achievements and spark celebration.

Phase 6, Waning Gibbous: Reflect and refine actions based on lessons learned. Draw on this waning phase to help sweep up after the party. The celebration is over—it's back to work, knowing fully what went well.

Phase 7, Last (Third) Quarter Moon: Acknowledge, release, and forgive. This phase offers the chance to acknowledge that life is not perfect, let go of any negativity holding you back, and forgive anyone and everyone you choose—even yourself!

Phase 8, Waning Crescent: The cycle ends—renew and reflect in quiet darkness. Listen to your heart and align your priorities. Wipe the slate clean—release and remove anything that does not fill you with energy and joy. Position yourself to begin a new phase with a new goal and a new attitude.

MINDFUL MEDITATION

Mindful meditation can ease stress, boost creativity, increase focus, and promote empathy—valuable life tools, indeed. Adding meditation to enhance magical living is not required, but it offers another tool to tap into your inner thoughts and feelings that can then become intentions set to achieve your goals.

Mindful meditation is the practice of being present, *in the moment*, and paying attention to your body, especially your breathing, emotions, sensations, and thoughts. When your mind wanders, and it will, recognize it and return your focus to your breath—all without judgment. Meditation is not about tuning out everything in our lives but, rather, tuning in to the present—the good, the bad, the happy, the sad—again, without judgment, and being with ourselves.

As with all things we learn, mindful meditation takes practice and consistency; even ten minutes a day can help. Once you begin to feel the benefits in your life, you will crave the quiet peace that meditation affords.

YOUR ALTAR

A magical toolkit is not required to live a magic-inspired life. But a few things can inspire your work and help improve your focus on energy vibrations to release your intentions into the Universe.

Though definitely not necessary, an altar provides a visual reminder and a physical space to focus your energy, meditate, or try a spell or two—inside or out. Consider setting up an altar as your place to visualize and set intentions for a life lived well. You can have more than one, each focused on a different purpose, like romance, or healthy living, or gratitude, for example.

An altar does not have to be fancy, and it can be as simple as a windowsill or cardboard box. It can even be a shelf or dresser top where you display your crystals, candles, or other reminders of your intentions so you are aware every day of the work you're doing to keep your home a thriving place.

Consider an altar by your bed with objects devoted to dreams and relaxation. Or one in your work area to boost creativity and energy. Or even in your garden to celebrate Nature and the charms and abundance she lends to your world.

Set up and decorate your altar any way you wish—be as fancy, creative, or minimalist as you like. As much as possible, keep the elements that make up your altar natural, for their innate, individual energies.

Your altar represents you: your home, heart, hopes, dreams, intentions, and life. If you stay true to those things, your altar will be ready to help you work your magic when called upon.

BELLS

The sound of tolling bells can be all at once haunting, soothing, celebratory, summoning, time-telling, and alarming. Their vibrational energies communicate messages that speak directly to us in mystical ways, and bells have been used for centuries for communication. They are also revered in many spiritual traditions—from Buddhism to Christianity—for their abilities in calling spirits to us and dispelling negative energies and lurking evil.

Witches like to hang small bells from doorknobs to dissuade evil spirits from entering spaces. Their ringing is also used to invoke spirits as part of ritual spellwork. The Tibetan singing bowl, a type of bell, produces soothing sonorous tones used in meditation practices.

Bells of any kind can be used to signal the beginning and end of any ritual or meditation, such as for calling in and sending out compassion. Use any bell, or none, in your magical explorations. If you decide to use one, choose one with a tone and pitch that speaks to you.

THE MAGIC OF MUSIC

As with the sounds of bells, music is not something we see, but its powerful vibrational energies can touch us physically and emotionally. We've all experienced the anecdotal moments of music affecting mood—music that's made you cry, laugh, tingle with excitement, or swoon with romance—and you likely have that favorite song you return to when you need a boost or reboot. But science actually tells us that *listening to music with the set intention of improving mood* can really make us happier.

Studies have also shown that music improves meditation; it doesn't matter if it's the sound of the surf, your favorite jazz, new age, country, opera, or classic rock. Music's vibrations affect our vibrations and can help clear emotional and physical blockages so positive energy once again flows freely.

A music-filled home also inspires physical movement, reduces stress, relaxes the body, promotes better sleep, eases depression, boosts verbal intelligence in children, and keeps our brains active—all components of magical living.

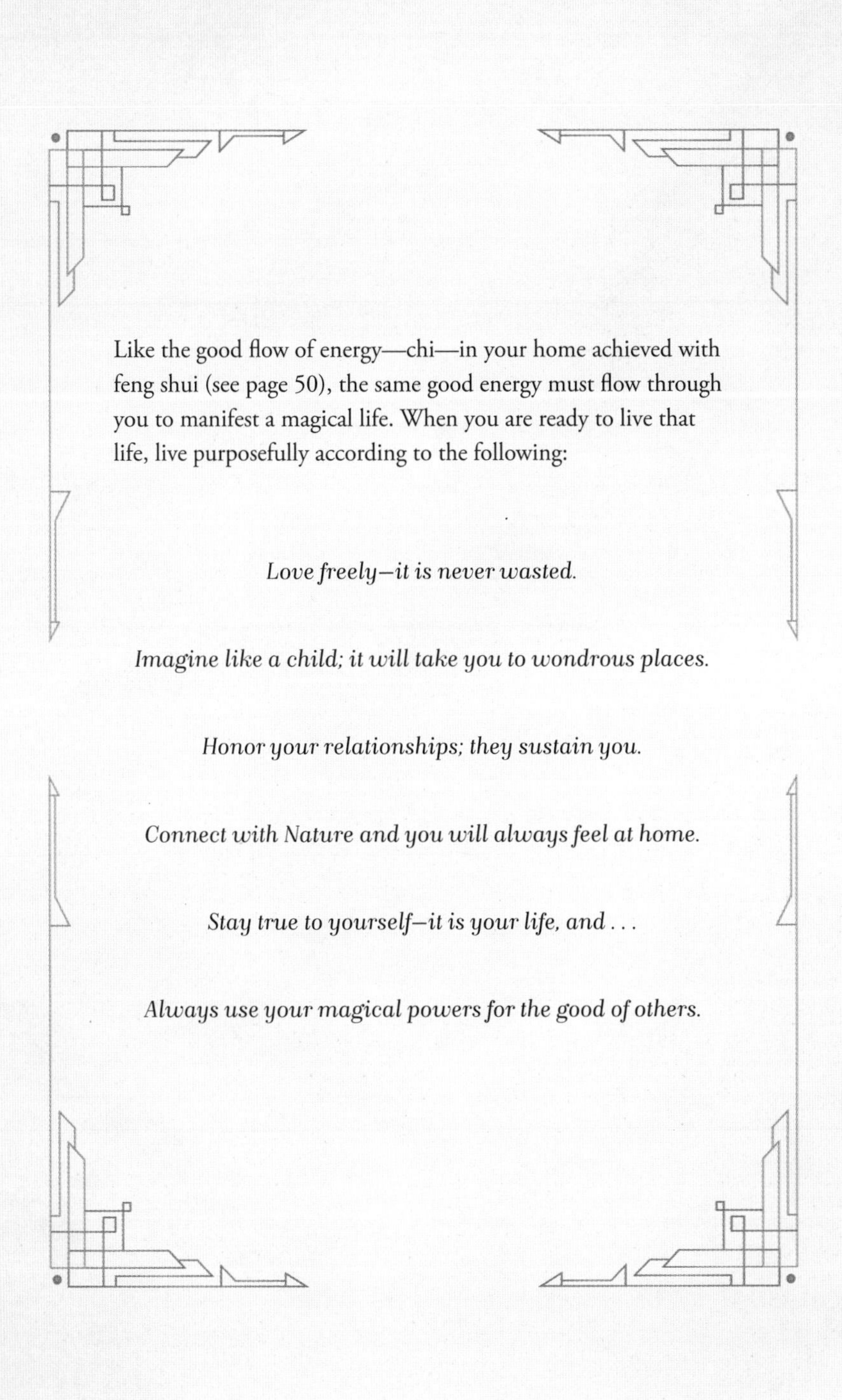

Like the good flow of energy—chi—in your home achieved with feng shui (see page 50), the same good energy must flow through you to manifest a magical life. When you are ready to live that life, live purposefully according to the following:

Love freely—it is never wasted.

Imagine like a child; it will take you to wondrous places.

Honor your relationships; they sustain you.

Connect with Nature and you will always feel at home.

Stay true to yourself—it is your life, and . . .

Always use your magical powers for the good of others.

BLESS THIS MAGICAL HOUSE

Blessed be. May all who enter be touched by life's good fortune.

Be it a palace or studio, high-rise or room to let, with new or inhabiting energies of the previous occupants, your house and home can be blessed to reset its energies, recharge its spirit, and protect against evil—and evict unwanted house-sitting spirits (see page 44) that may be more mischief than merry. Clear your house of any negative influence to allow positive energy to enter and make your home feel more abundant, loving, and sacred.

You'll want to clean and cleanse the house to begin. In this way, you can push "restart" on the energies in your home . . . cleaning out the negative and inviting in the positive. If it's a new home, a simple sweeping and Sage Smudging Ritual (see page 116) is perfect. If it's a home you've lived in for a while, declutter as much as you can, wash things like bed linens, curtains, and carpets and sweep, dust, and vacuum the rest. Pay attention to windows, as well, to invite the Sun's healing rays, the winds soothing hymns, and the Moon's glorious wisdom to pour into your space and fill it with the warmth and energy of life.

HOUSE BLESSING OR HOUSEWARMING?

A house blessing is usually done on or before moving into a new home. The tradition dates back centuries and often has a religious aspect to it with the purpose of warding off evil spirits. Here, "blessing" means removing negative energies to allow space for clean, positive intentions to fill in, for a life well lived and loved in this space.

A house blessing can be a simple, private occasion or blended with the traditional housewarming party which is more of a social gathering to introduce friends and extended family—even new neighbors—to your new home.

If it's a housewarming you want, take a cue from the early origins of this tradition and light a candle on your first night in the home (light just one or many in a variety of colors). Or choose the color based on which of the home's energies you'd like to heighten or calm (see page 14).

The purpose of early housewarmings was just as the name suggests: to warm the house. Invited guests brought gifts of wood to the new home, where it was used to stoke the fire in the fireplace. The house, thus warmed, was also the perfect setting for a celebratory meal to be shared, ensuring prosperity and abundance for all.

To prepare your space, let's start with the entrance—the place where the people you love, and those who bring positive loving energy into your home, enter. Create a magical welcome just by clearing the space.

BROOMS

The broom is an ancient tool used not only to keep dwellings clean, but also, historically, courtyards, roads, etc., for others to be able to pass by and enjoy. It also holds spiritual roots, with many believing in its powers to sweep away the bad as well as past evils that still haunt.

The besom broom, one of the earliest brooms, was a simple bundle of twigs or herbs gathered and attached to a handle. These brooms were often hung—bristles up—near doorways to guard against evil entering a home and to protect all inside.

When one thinks "broom," one often thinks "witch," and the besom broom is one of the most-associated symbols of Wicca. This traditional broom of witches was typically made from a bundle of birch twigs fastened to an oak or ash handle with willow wraps. It was used as a form of protection, whether from people or for spaces, and to sweep away any negative energies when preparing for spellwork.

An old African American tradition teaches that holding a broom above a newly married couple's heads protects them from future evil—and if that same couple jumps the broom, it is said to increase fertility.

English tradition says common law marriage is signified by jumping the broom.

Early Celtic pagans associated the broom with woodland faeries, seeking their magical help and wisdom in finding the best wood for the broom, knowing its enchantment was then guaranteed.

A broom placed across a doorway can protect your home against evil that may have been cast in your direction. But a broom that falls across a doorway foretells of an upcoming journey.

A broom works as a magical tool, able to dispel negative energies, as well as dirt and dust that are just plain negative. Finding a handmade broom of natural materials is a plus. It vibrates with the good energies of those materials. When moving into a new space, ditch your old broom and the detritus it contains for a new one and a clean sweep!

Finish the job by setting out a new WELCOME mat, if you can, or sweeping the outside of the entryway clean. Wash any glass in the entryway, such as a glass door or the window in your door, to let the energizing sunshine through.

Next, pick a room. Which room do you spend the most time in? Which room has a "bad vibe" when you walk into it now? That's the place to start (and you don't have to clean the whole room at once). Get rid of what does not serve you well—old clothes, old pictures, broken items, dirty dishes, etc. Dust, sweep, or vacuum. Clean any dirty surfaces, using natural cleaners wherever you can, not only for your benefit but also to care for our Earth, giving us so much for which to be thankful.

Open the windows and let the stale, negative energy out and the clean, refreshing energy in. Spritz that sage cleansing spray and take a deep breath. Thank your cleaning tools for helping you complete the task and feel the clean energizing aura fill you from head to toe. Repeat with other rooms in the home, as needed.

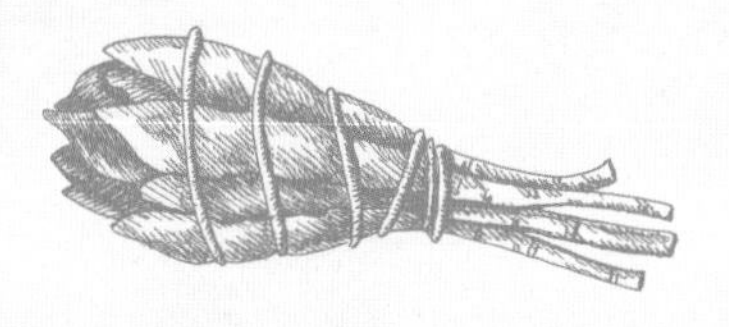

HOME CLEANING TIPS

Whether you just want to create a calm, stress-free place to be or dive deeper into magical workings in your home, doing so in a clean, fresh space feels so much better, and it changes the energy of the space in which you're working for the better.

As there is only so much time in a day (and how much of it do you really want to spend cleaning?) start slowly and keep at it. Before you know it, you'll be whistling a happy tune for no reason at all.

One thing at a time.

Some cleaning tips to help keep your home in tip-top magical condition:

- **Bathrooms** are spaces where we cleanse, renew, and refresh ourselves. Consider the bathroom a top priority to keep organized and fresh. Adding lavender-scented items will help calm; pine adds an air of freshness to energize; and citrus aromas can help lighten and brighten a mood and put a spring in your step for the day.
- **The kitchen** is often the heart of the home. As we learn from Vesta (see page 46), tending the home fires is constant work. Think smart when tending to your kitchen space. Clean as you go. Keep things neat and tidy, if not spic and span. The everyday smells of a kitchen in action are enough to provoke deep and meaningful memories. Cook for those you love, or love those who cook for you! Keep fresh flowers on the table, when you are able, to invite in Nature's beauty and add a touch of the calming outdoors.
- **Bedrooms** provide rest, renewal, romance, and retreat. Make them a space you want to spend time in. Declutter, banish electronics, and only use the space for sleep or romance—no eating, work, bill paying, etc.

Use the power of scent in any room for an instant lift or mood twist. Diffuse essential oils (see page 84) or make a homemade potpourri (see page 89) to sprinkle beautiful scents that reflect your intentions anywhere you desire—your very own fairy dust.

HOUSEWARMING AND WELCOMING TRADITIONS

The beauty of a housewarming party is you can make it into whatever suits your style. Really, all you need are a few like-minded friends and family to imbue your house with love and good wishes.

Here are a few traditions passed down through the years that show the common factor is love.

- In the Philippines, it's a tradition to scatter coins around the living room when first moving into a new home. Wealth and prosperity will reign. Others place them under the carpet, embed them into the walk leading to the house, or even build them into the foundation, which also attracts house spirits (see page 44) to your dwelling to serve and protect the family within.
- In Russian tradition, it is customary to welcome someone into a new home with gifts of bread, wine, and salt: bread so that there is no hunger; salt so that life is full-flavored; and wine for great joy.

- In the Southern United States, in a tradition thought to have originated in South Carolina, painting a porch ceiling blue, specifically Haint Blue, was a way to deter restless spirits (Haints)—still walking Earth—from your home. This soft blue-green color protecting homes from evil spirits is also seen on doors and windowsills guarding those entrances from harm. Any color blue will do, and it invites the sky in.
- With its roots in old eighteenth-century French tradition, the trammel, or pot hook, was typically the last item placed in a new home—in the fireplace. Tradition held that a pot was then placed on the trammel and a meal cooked to thank all who helped build the new home! Another reason to bring food, wine, or water to a housewarming party today.
- The pot placed on the trammel was typically a cauldron, a heavy metal cooking vessel in which the meal was cooked. Cauldrons throughout the centuries have held both magical witch connotations and a relationship to the hearth in many cultures. As the vehicle for providing nourishment, it is a symbol of abundance and can be seen to represent transformation and rebirth. If you don't have need of a cauldron to cook with, place it on your altar filled with fresh flowers or candles, or make an offering to the house goddess in it, or fill with water to divine the future (see Scrying, page 99).

PROTECT AND BRING LUCK TO THIS MAGICAL HOUSE

May those who enter this house live life fully without illness or fear.

The home provides a cloak of protection for all those within and forms a physical barrier to keep elements out. The spiritual elements, however, were feared to enter through open portals, like chimneys, doors, and windows. Hence, protective and magical symbols and offerings were frequently placed in those spots to repel, prevent, or guard against unwanted spiritual harm. Protection magic is one of the oldest forms of spellwork.

Keeping the home sacred, happy, and protected from evil influences, arising from fears of the unknown, is as old as history. Your home is your sacred space: the place you live, raise a family, nurture, and grow into your best version of you. It is the one place you want to keep shielded from anything evil that may want to enter and cause chaos. Magical symbols that bring a little luck and protection to your home will keep you and your loved ones as safe as possible.

We'll explore other ways to use your magical living space to live a joyful life, but our first task is keeping it safe from harm. If you feel any negativity surrounding you, your loved ones, or your home, use these magical charms and symbols to keep evil away.

CHARMING SYMBOLS, HOUSEHOLD SPIRITS, AND MAGICAL LORE

Charming traditions abound from different cultures and religions to bless your space and keep it safe. Charming symbols were used for centuries for protection from evil spirits and as an invitation for good luck to take up residence. Symbols of protection can be found drawn on walls, carved into stone or jewels, fashioned into talismans, hung for decoration, or used for adoration. Take your pick from some highlighted here and work with what resonates for you. Research specific symbols that may be native to your heritage or spiritual beliefs as well.

DREAM CATCHER

The dream catcher is a powerful protective symbol to Native American peoples and dates back centuries to the Ojibwe tribe, for whom natural elements were supremely important and viewed as profound teachers.

Comprising a circle made of willow onto which is woven a web of sinew and to which feathers are attached, dream catchers would have been made by the women of the tribe to protect infants and children. Suspended above their cradles, dream catchers allowed good dreams to pass through the web and travel down the feathers to the sleeping child. Bad dreams, however, became entangled in the web, where they would stay until evaporated in the morning light.

Dream catchers can protect adults and children alike from receiving messages meant to lead us astray or do harm.

To honor and respect the Native American symbolism and culture, look for original Native American–made dream catchers to use in your home, or find ones made of all-natural materials to honor Nature as teacher and reap the rewards of their vibrational powers.

EYE OF HORUS

From jewelry and tattoos to tote bags and playing cards, there is no lack of ways to carry a little extra protection with you or safeguard your home. The Eye of Horus is an ancient Egyptian symbol. Horus, the son of Isis and Osiris who is often depicted with the head of a peregrine falcon, is said to have lost an eye—his left—in a battle with his uncle, who had killed his father. (His right eye is known as the Eye of Ra, the Sun god.) Horus's left eye is also associated with the waxing and waning of the Moon, another magical tool whose energies and phases can offer protection. Today, the all-seeing Eye of Horus is said to offer great power and protection as well as healing.

HAMSA

The Hamsa is a powerful Middle Eastern symbol of protection and guardian against the Evil Eye and other evil spells. It can have various meanings in different religious interpretations, but the common thread is protection. It is also believed to bestow health, happiness, and luck upon its bearer.

HORSESHOE

Hanging an iron horseshoe—preferably used—above your front door (or in some homes, over the kitchen entryway) was believed to bring good luck and protect the inhabitants of the house from evil.

Irish legend holds that, somewhere around the tenth century, Dunstan, a bishop and blacksmith, met the Devil himself, who demanded a horseshoe. Dunstan complied, making one, fresh and hot, and nailed it to the Devil's foot. Howling ensued, as did begging to remove it. "On one condition," said Dunstan. "You must respect the horseshoe at all times and never enter any space bearing its sign." The Devil agreed, and a tradition of "horseshoe as protector" was born.

Considering that iron itself is thought to be a lucky material due to its "magical" ability to survive fire, (and the blacksmith occupation is also a lucky one) the horseshoe is thrice-powered to protect. Hang it open-end up, or open-end down. Open-end up means fill this house with luck. Open-end down means let luck rain out and down!

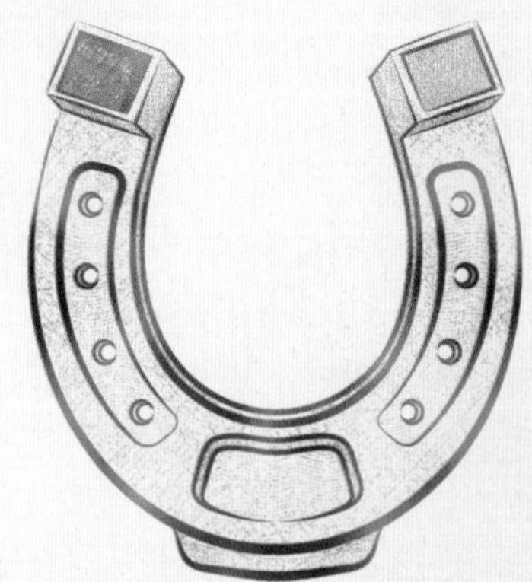

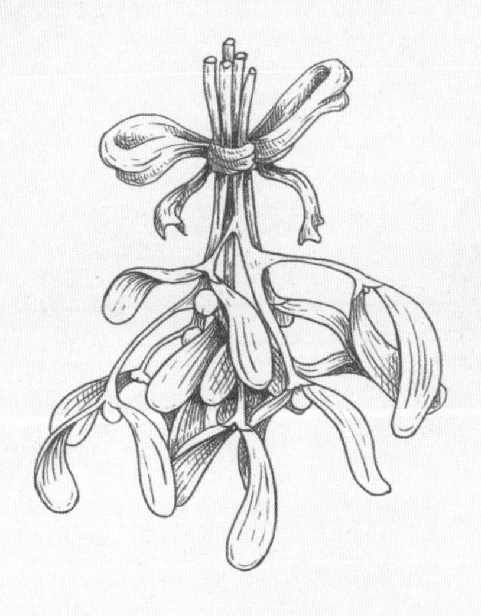

MISTLETOE

Typically confined to the category of Christmas decorations, mistletoe grows wild and abundant in many countries—and in difficult climates. Its evergreen leaves symbolize life. In the language of flowers (see page 77), mistletoe signifies strength and the ability to surmount difficult odds.

The ancient Celtic Druids observed mistletoe blossoming—even through winter—and held sacred its life-affirming abilities. They also believed strongly in its protective charms. So, hang it freely throughout your home to protect the love nurtured there and any children at home, attract luck and good fortune, stimulate fertility, and ward off evil spirits. Be forewarned: refusing a kiss under the mistletoe is said to bring bad luck—so don't undo all the good you've been working to achieve with mistletoe's mysterious gifts.

NOTE: Mistletoe can be poisonous to pets, so please do not leave it anywhere they can access it.

PENTAGRAM

The very recognizable symbol of Wicca, the pentacle, features a five-pointed star enclosed in a circle. The points represent Nature's elements—earth, air, fire, and water—with the fifth point, at the top of the star, representing the spirit of the Universe, the energy of all things. It is an ancient and powerful symbol of protection.

TRIQUETRA

Triquetra translates as "three-cornered." The triquetra symbol, though often identified with pagan Celtic culture, has been found in various cultures and locations going back more than 5,000 years. Its true origins appear to be uncertain. The Celtic connection likely arises from its appearance in the gloriously illustrated *Book of Kells*, a circa eighth-century manuscript containing the four gospels of the New Testament and other religious texts.

This symbol variously represents the Father, Son, and Holy Ghost to Christians; maiden, mother, and crone to pagans; air, water, and earth as the exalted elements of Nature; past, present, and future; and, when it includes a circle binding everything together, everlasting love and life, among many symbols celebrating the power of "three."

You can find this symbol on household items like trivets, jewelry, carvings, and prints to use and display throughout your home where you may want to boost its personal protective powers.

VIKING RUNES

The Vikings, seafaring warriors who left their homelands in search of fertile land and wealth, were said to be illiterate. Not so, entirely—they had their own way of communicating with runes.

The ancient Viking runes are a pictorial alphabet of sorts, which legend holds were discovered by Odin, chief among the Norse gods. Each symbol or rune, is a visual representation of a sound and functions like a letter in the alphabet. The twenty-four runes, when used together, formed the basis of a language for communication between people.

Additionally, each individual rune was thought to hold some secret power—potent enough to change life. Just writing that rune—usually carved in a hard substance, such as rock, wood, stone, or gemstone—could invoke that magic from above. There were even rune masters called in to interpret the runes and predict the future. The origin of the word *rune* means "mystery" or "magic."

Magical Rune Symbols

In addition to symbolic jewelry, intention-driven decorative artifacts for your home, and even mysterious tattoos, rune tiles—made of stone, wood, or glass—are available in sets and can be used like tarot cards to divine the future. Or you can select a tile at random and meditate on it daily to set your intentions.

However runes speak to you, they are powerful symbols from a powerful people and tradition. Heed their messages well. The symbols from this runic alphabet, the elder futhark, dates from the first to eighth centuries CE, and their meanings come to us through the medieval Rune Poems, from England, Iceland, and Norway.

ᚠ **FEHU:** fire, fulfillment in all aspects of life, wealth preservation

ᚢ **URUZ:** home, rebirth, strength of will

ᚦ **THURISAZ:** contemplation, patience in decision making, potential danger

ᚨ **ANSUZ:** prosperity; receiving messages, gifts, or intuition

ᚱ **RAIDHO:** communication, journey, movement, work

ᚲ **KAUNAN:** clarity, dispelling darkness, wisdom

ᚷ **GEBO:** generosity, partnership

ᚹ **WUNJO:** joy

ᚺ **HAGALAZ:** change, destruction, growth, loss

ᚾ **NAUDHIZ:** need, unfulfilled desire, reassessment of plans

JERA: harvest, rewards reaped from hard work

EIHWAZ: strength, stability

NAME UNKNOWN: mystery

NAME UNKNOWN: protection from enemies

SOWILO: positive energy, solace

TIWAZ: victory, honor

BERKANAN: fertility, health, growth

EHWAZ: duality, companionship, trust

MANNAZ: humanity, support

LAGUZ: ebb and flow, water, emotions

INGWAZ: fertilization, manifestation, the beginning of something

OTHALAN: goddess, heritage, inheritance, legacy, tradition

DAGAZ: breakthrough, hope

WIND CHIMES

Wind chimes and their ethereal tones have charmed us the world over for centuries. Their soothing sounds can calm a weary soul. The use of wind chimes can be dated back to places such as ancient Greece and Rome, Southeast Asia, and China, where their presence has been interpreted to warn away evil spirits and invite good spirits in, as well as the more practical purpose of warning away hungry critters from crops. The Chinese believe the chimes connect people who hear them to Earth and establish a sense of being present in the moment, which leads to increased well-being.

Feng shui (see page 50) followers revere the wind chime for its ability to calm and soothe the home environment. Hang wind chimes near the front and back doors (but far enough away that they do not hit the door, or your guests!) where their ancient customs of warning away evil spirits still live, and they can welcome guests and gentle spirits inside.

Outside a window or on a porch are also magical locations, as they catch the breeze and fill your home with their spirit-lifting song, which is believed to reduce stress and encourage relaxation. While traditionally hung outside where the chimes can join in harmony with the wind, wind chimes are also suitable for shifting energies indoors. Look for those made of natural materials, such as crystals, sea glass, or seashells.

WISHBONE: WHAT A LUCKY BREAK!

The wishbone—a symbol of luck and wishes granted—is a mainstay today of Easter, Thanksgiving, and Christmas meals. The turkey wishbone has, for generations, delighted children by granting a wish to the lucky one breaking off the larger piece—using pinkies only, please. It is believed the bone's good luck attributes were ascribed by the Etruscans, dating to between the eighth and third centuries BCE. The Etruscans believed birds—the wishbone's source—could foretell the future. So, whether decorating or dining with the wishbone, take a moment to thank the, rather less lucky, turkey or goose for providing the wonderful meal and be grateful for this granter of wishes.

WREATHS

The wreath, an unending circle, symbolizes eternity. Hanging a wreath on a door can also be an invitation for luck to come calling. Made from natural materials such as herbs, twigs, flowers, and more, the wreath has served many purposes through time. Pagans celebrated winter solstice—that time when the tide turns toward spring—with Yule ceremonies, including a wreath representing spring and the cycle of the seasons. Dating back to the Persian empire and ancient Greece, floral and jewel-studded wreaths adorned the heads of royalty and other powerful citizens to project their status to society.

Evergreen wreaths decorating graves marked the circle of eternal life, and they are placed there even today to honor the dead. Ancient Greeks and Romans revered the laurel and olive wreaths as signs of victory and honor. They were given to victorious Olympic athletes and worn by returning courageous warriors and politicians claiming power. Wreaths hung on doors announced the occupants' victories. The traditional Christmas wreath is not only a welcoming sign of the holiday season but also, serving as the Advent wreath, symbolizes the coming of Christ to Christians the world over.

Wreaths are also displayed for their decorative touch. Choose one made of natural materials to add vibrational energy to your home, or tuck some fresh or dried herbs and flowers into one to add a bit of magic to any room in your home.

HOUSEHOLD SPIRITS AND MAGICAL LORE

Many cultures throughout history have depended on house spirits for domestic help and protection. Whether household spirits or goddesses of the Earth, these protective beings who hail from the Earth and plant kingdoms guard, defend, cast good luck upon—and sometimes tidy up around—the home. Sometimes attached to a whole family and sometimes just an individual family member, these spirits are industrious and steadfast in their duties.

When household duties weigh you down, take a few moments to connect with one of these spirits and ask for help. Better yet, take stock of your situation and invite one into your home. They take up little room—and a little respect for their individual quirks, plus some food, drink, and comfort, are all they seek in return for spreading good luck and providing protection to your home and family.

BEAN-TIGHE

From Britain and Ireland we meet Bean-Tighe, a benevolent old woman with a people-pleasing personality, who is happiest when busy at work. She gravitates toward the elderly and single mothers who need help with the children. After a busy day of keeping the home tidy, she can be found tucking the family, including the pets, into bed and lulling them off to dreamland. Rumor in the fairy kingdom says strawberries and sweet cream are a particular weakness for this fairy godmother–like sprite.

BRIGID

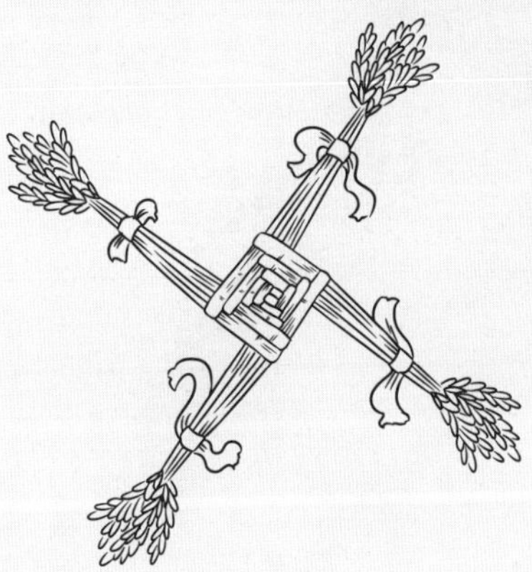

The Gaelic goddess of the hearth, whose name means "exalted one," was patron of the sacred household fires. Tradition held that the woman of the house, while performing the daily chore of putting the fire to bed for the evening, pleaded with Brigid for protection of all who dwelt within. Brigid also represents the fires of creativity.

Tales are told of St. Brigid weaving a cross from rushes as she calmed the restless soul of a chieftain who lay dying. Hanging a replica of St. Brigid's cross on your front door or entryway is thought to protect your home from evil spirits and fire and ward off hunger in the home.

BROWNIE

Long recounted in English and Scottish tales, the Brownie, or Hob, is a solitary little home fairy. This seldom-seen but oft-heard gnome-like spirit loves the rural dwelling or farm where he can help the mistress of the house by sweeping and cleaning and tending to chores to his heart's content . . . usually at night under cover of darkness. While industrious and clearly talented, the Brownie can be temperamental. If it's dirt your home needs protection from or animals that need feeding, leave out some sweet milk or cream, or even cake, to entice this fine fellow in.

Beware his cousin, the Hobgoblin, though, who is only out for mischief—at your home's expense! If this fate befalls you, make the gift of clothes to set him free.

DOMOVOI

Master of the house . . . oh, you thought that was you? Well, he'll let you think that. Descending from Slavic tradition, this otherworldly house sprite, like the Brownie, attaches to a family and, when in a good mood, will faithfully serve and protect. Keep him happy, though, or mischief ensues. He is particularly fond of children and pets. The Domovoi takes his mission to protect the home from spiritual and physical harm seriously.

The few who have seen him say he is a hairy, scary, frightening little figure. The Domovoi prefers to stay out of sight. His presence is felt long before he is seen. Misplaced your keys? Hearing footsteps at night? Animals are active? (Probably the Domovoi!)

The Domovoi is happiest when the home is in order; he dislikes a mess and is offended by harsh language. He appreciates a moment of silent acknowledgment when you are away from home. A light supper of milk and bread, or leftovers, is appreciated, too.

FRIGG

Associated with domesticity and all it affords—love, marriage, motherhood, and nurturing—Frigg: Norse goddess extraordinaire and wife of Odin, who is the all-father and most powerful Norse god—is the chief maternal officer. In her powerful position as Odin's wife, she may sit on the high throne, with Odin, where she has a magnificent view of the world. Here, she can see far into the future, yet, wisely, does not reveal all she sees. Seek her wisdom in matters of hearth and home and invite her in anytime your goddess energies are running low.

GABIJA

Lithuanian goddess of the home fires and guardian of the home and family, like the Greek goddess Hestia (below), Gabija is charged with tending the flame that is the center of the home. In Lithuanian tradition, a new bride is given fire from her mother's hearth to ignite her own home fires, ensuring an auspicious start to her new married life. Bearing the strength of the element of fire, Gabija's powers are greatly respected. She is prayed to for protection of the home and family and kept satisfied with offerings of bread.

HESTIA/VESTA

The Greek goddess Hestia (or Vesta, to the Romans) was a virgin goddess dedicated to the hearth, home, family, and community. The original domestic goddess, this kind and forgiving figure was widely worshipped and held sacred in the home, where she tended the unending hearth fires—to warm, nourish, and sustain. Offerings of wine and food in her honor were common. Though Hestia had no children of her own, new family members were presented to her at the hearth for her blessing and welcomed into the home. Offer a toast at dinner in thanks for her steadfastness.

TRASGU

Spanish lore gives us their equivalent of the Irish leprechaun, a lovably mischievous red hat–wearing sprite who, once tamed, becomes a loyal household helper. Don't expect complete domesticity, though; a bit of unruliness is part of life. He is difficult to be rid of, so treat him well and enjoy the benefits of the nightly chores he tackles.

ZASHIKI WARASHI

These adorable house spirits hail from Japan's Iwate prefecture. They are vigilant guardians of the home and said to be bearers of good luck. Though seldom seen—usually only by a homeowner or children in the home—and appearing as young children, they are often heard instead: they love a good prank—your first indication that zashiki warashi have settled in may be a child's powdery footprints all over the house.

Zashiki warashi usually take up residence in a guest room and love to amuse children. Elderly and childless couples love them as their own. Their presence in a house foretells of fortune and success, and their home guardianship is so valued that they are eagerly courted. Offerings of food and drink, as well as coins built into a new home's foundation, are said to be attractive to the zashiki warashi. If one befriends your home, count your blessings.

CREATE A HARMONIZING HOME

May this home be a haven of abundant peace and creative joy.

Paying attention to your energy reserves, practicing self-care, and being in tune and present with Nature and its energies are guiding principles to living a magic-filled life. This extends to your home, too. As you know, your home has its own vibrational energies; keeping them positive and in tip-top shape will only enhance your magical living.

Here we'll look at that energy as applied by the ancient Chinese practice of feng shui to harmonize your home and life. Feng shui is an ancient Chinese practice dating back thousands of years. It is based on the principle of *chi,* or energy, and its ability to flow freely in your home. *Feng shui* literally translates as "wind-water"—two of Nature's flowing energies—and is concerned with living in harmony with Nature and your environment. This is accomplished through placement—of objects, color, light—to maximize the flow of chi and anchor the energy.

Feng shui touches all aspects of life in your home: career, creativity, self, friends, family, children, travel, health, wealth, reputation, and romantic relationships. The ancient feng shui masters were far ahead of scientific times in their understanding that all things in life are made of energy and those energies vibrate at different frequencies. As we, too, are made of energy, we are bound to the rest of the world in this way, and all energies—as they shift, meet, and change—affect each other.

FENG SHUI ELEMENTAL TOOLS

For indoor spaces to recreate the chi of the outdoors, feng shui and other Eastern philosophies consider five natural elements and their unique energies as vital to their magical toolkit: *wood, fire, earth, metal,* and *water*. Each must be present for harmony and balance to exist. The correct blend of these elements creates harmonious surroundings.

Understanding how these elements work together helps you understand how they can work in your home. They have the potential to work well together—creating good harmony, or a creative cycle—or they can clash and create cacophony, or a destructive cycle.

In the creative cycle:

Wood creates fire | fire (as ash) creates earth | earth supports metal | metal supports water | water supports wood

This is the cycle you strive to achieve. Understanding the opposite, destructive cycle, can help you solve the problem of a room that just doesn't work or promote peace.

In the destructive cycle:

Wood weakens earth | earth weakens water | water extinguishes fire | fire destroys metal | metal damages wood

You don't need to start from scratch to make a more balanced, harmonious space, nor do you need to be a master of feng shui rules. As with all things magical, start small and only do what speaks to you.

BAGUA MAP

Combining the natural elements, their energies, and color leads us to the bagua map, a nine-quadrant map that helps you establish the power of your intentions in your home. Whether you want to nurture love, health, money, wisdom, or more, this ancient tool can guide you. As with all things requiring time and energy, concentrating on one or two places in your home at one time keeps your energy focused for better outcomes.

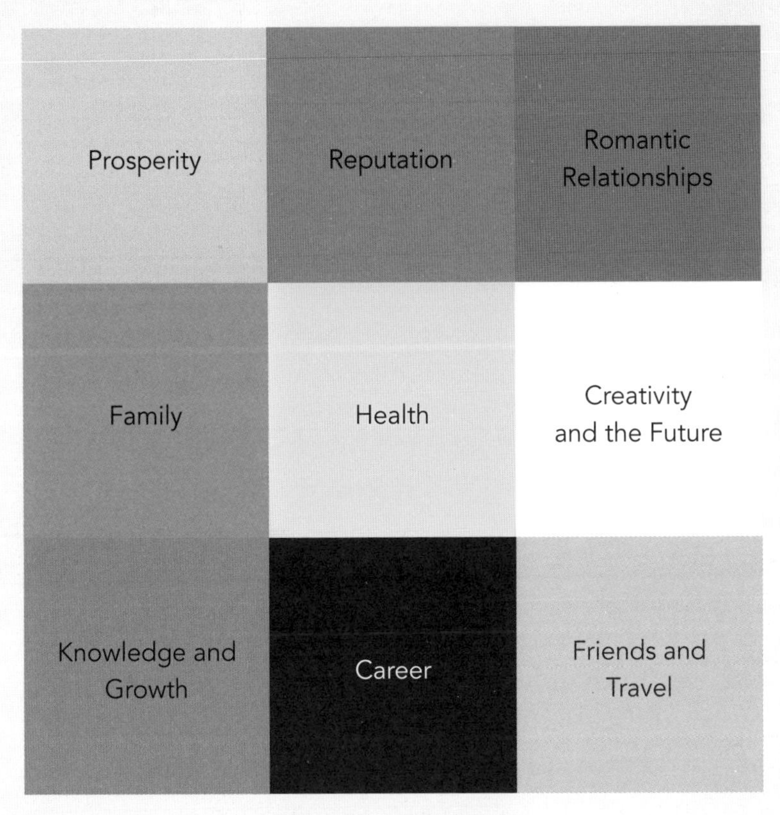

Orient the map so the bottom lines up with your home's entrance and visualize the map corresponding to your home's floor plan as if you have placed it on your home from above to identify the power areas of the home.

You can also align the map with *just one room*: align the bottom of the map with the room's doorway, or primary doorway, as you did with the whole house. This allows you to focus on particular areas within one room that may need special attention.

Refer to the following chart to see which element may also correspond to these energies as well as colors and shapes.

And remember, *ALWAYS* follow your instincts. Do what feels right for you in your home, and incorporate some whimsy and fun into the process along the way!

BLENDING THE ELEMENTS

Bagua Map Energy Location: *Family*

Element: Wood

Energy: Abundance, growth, new beginnings, new life, vitality

Counters: Feeling stuck or confused, low energy

Colors: Brown, green, blues

Shapes: Rectangular, vertical shapes

Bagua Map Energy Location: *Reputation*

Element: Fire

Energy: Heat of passion, romance, life, success, Sun's energy

Counters: Lack of creativity, loneliness, low energy

Colors: Bright pink, orange, red, yellow

Shapes: Star, triangular shapes

Bagua Map Energy Location: *Health*

Element: Earth

Energy: Centered feelings, emotional and physical health; nourishment, stability, support

Counters: Feelings of being ungrounded, lack of stability

Colors: Earth tones, yellows

Shapes: Squares

Bagua Map Energy Location*: Creativity and the Future*

Element: Metal

Energy: Children, clarity, freshness, joy, purity

Counters: Frustration, lack of energy

Colors: Gray, metallic finishes, white

Shapes: Rounds

Bagua Map Energy Location*: Career*

Element: Water

Energy: Abundance, calm, ease, flowing of wealth, journey of life

Counters: Poor health, stagnation, stress

Colors: Black, blue

Shapes: Curves, flowing shapes

Bagua Map Energy Location: ***Prosperity***

Elements: Water, wood

Energy: Abundance, gratitude, wealth

Counters: Selfishness

Colors: Gold, purple

Shapes: Curves, flowing shapes, rectangles

Bagua Map Energy Location*: Romantic Relationships*

Element: Fire

Energy: Care for the environment, loving relationships, self-care

Counters: Apathy

Colors: Pink, purple, red, rose

Shapes: Star, triangular shapes

Bagua Map Energy Location: ***Friends and Travel***

Elements: Earth, metal

Energy: Gratitude, help, open, relationships

Counters: Loneliness, selfishness, stagnation

Colors: Grays, pastels

Shapes: Round, square shapes

Bagua Map Energy Location: ***Knowledge and Growth***

Elements: Earth, fire

Energy: Inspiration, wisdom

Counters: Lack of balance and boundaries, lack of progress

Colors: Earth tones, orange, red, turquoise, yellow

Shapes: Stars, square shapes

LET'S FENG SHUI!

Before you dive in, take a moment to set your course. As with everything magical, you need to be clear and firm on your intentions. If you have not set any yet, now is the time to do so. The energy-filled practice of feng shui combines the energies of your home, the items in your home, and your intentions to produce a magical environment for living your best life.

With energies swirling, you may wonder how to keep things under control. Feng shui has an answer: the **command position**. Being in command means being mistress of your own energies, to be most effective in any situation—with whatever energies are present. As with all things magical, only the good is the focus here; this is not about commanding or controlling others.

Finding the command position in any space is easy: it is the spot in a room farthest from and opposite (not directly aligned with it, but where you can see) the door. Positioned here, you have a view of your kingdom—or room—and are prepared for all that enters.

While the command position alone offers strength, it does require some backup. So, for instance, in your most vulnerable room, the bedroom, positioning the bed against a wall, where you can see the door but are not directly aligned with it, puts you in the command position. But, if there are windows in the wall, your position is weakened. Close the shades or move the bed to a solid wall for the most control. Consider this when evaluating the command position for the rooms, or spots in a room, where you spend the most time.

DECLUTTERING IS MORE THAN TIDYING UP

Just as we seek to declutter our minds from stress and negative self-talk, *clutter is negative self-talk for your house*. Remove it and improve your well-being. Once finished, take a moment to just sit, be still, be grateful. Breathe and thank your home for its shelter. Focus on your breath and let the mind's clutter dissolve in the mist.

FENG SHUI BY ROOM

Pick one room or tackle them all, if you wish. I recommend starting with the entry, the energy portal to your home, then moving to rooms or spaces you avoid or don't spend a lot of time in because of their bad energy vibes.

ENTRY

Clearing, cleaning, or redecorating your home's front entrance has a calming and welcoming effect. It sets the tone for your home. Paint your front door. Feng shui principles assign specific colors to attract good luck to your home, depending on the direction the door faces. If your door looks:

North, choose black or blue

South, boast red or orange

West, display white or gray

East, tint brown or green

LIVING SPACES: LIVING ROOM, FAMILY ROOM

With a few feng shui suggestions, you can create a welcoming gathering space for friends and family. Clean the windows and do not block the view. Place the sofa in a command position against a solid wall. Strive to incorporate rounded furniture into the room to ease the energy flow. Paint the walls based either on the energies reflected in the room's placement vis-à-vis the bagua map or on the intentions you've set for the space.

Use brown- and green-colored objects (rugs, curtains, pillows, botanical prints), including plants and wooden items. Display family photos, of both current and deceased family members.

HOME OFFICE

Create a space for disciplined and creative work. Place your desk in a command position. Add a touch of greenery. Plants with rounded leaves, such as the jade plant, are said to bring luck and prosperity. Any principle of joyful living dictates separating your home office from your home life. If you can't set a physical boundary, like locating your office in a separate room with a door, set up a screen or curtain to close off the space. Avoid overcrowded bookshelves to avoid jumbling your mind.

Incorporate the element of fire to ignite success: a lit fireplace, if you're lucky enough to have one in this room, or candles carefully tended, and pictures of sunsets or other red accessories.

KITCHEN

Your kitchen is the heart of your home and the place from which your family's energy flows. It also contains all the vital feng shui elements: wood, fire, earth, metal, and water. Keep it open and well tended. Keep the stove and counters clean and tidy. Make sure everything in the kitchen works. Recycle or donate items you do not use. As the kitchen is the metaphorical center of the home according to the bagua map, incorporate crystals and stones, celebrate the empty spaces, and display pottery pieces you adore using.

BEDROOM

We spend a lot of time in our bedrooms, and with good feng shui, the space can promote rest and peaceful sleep. Place the bed in a command position with the headboard against a solid wall, if possible, to keep energies from flowing over your head and disrupting sleep. Make your bed at the start of each day. Keep the room clean and uncluttered, including under the bed! Leave space on both sides of the bed for balance. Avoid mirrors in this room, if you can, which reflect and heighten energy.

BATHROOM

The focus on life-giving water makes this room especially nourishing and deserving of attention. Paint the room in hues of blue, green, or white, or a combination. Keep the air in the room fresh and flowing. Add some wooden elements (water supports wood), including in the form of woody plants, for a touch of healing Nature, which also helps purify the air. Add your favorite crystal energy. *Keep the toilet lid down!*

CLOSETS

Show your closets some tough love. If there is no room for anything else there, you are living a cramped, stressed life. Declutter with a keen eye and donate appropriately to charity.

GARDEN

Applying feng shui principles to your garden creates a peaceful, inviting place where you can reap the benefits of chi energy and Nature's soothing charms. If you don't have a garden, tend to a porch, patio, balcony, or windowsill.

As inside the house, keep the garden uncluttered: remove dead plants, fallen limbs, or twigs, and keep pathways clear. Add a water element such as a birdbath or wind chimes (see page 42). Balance the elements of wood, fire, earth, metal, and water; place each item in the garden with a purpose and element in mind. Create winding paths to enhance energy flow.

GARAGE

Yes, your garage can also get the feng shui treatment. Start with decluttering. There is probably lots of stuff in there you've completely forgotten about. Remove it and organize the space so it can be used for its real purpose—storing your car. Sweep the floor.

When you've finished preparing the garage and are ready to park the car in it, clean out your car while you're at it. Throw away trash or remove items you don't need. Refresh the air with a car aromatherapy diffuser. Wash the windows and vacuum the interior.

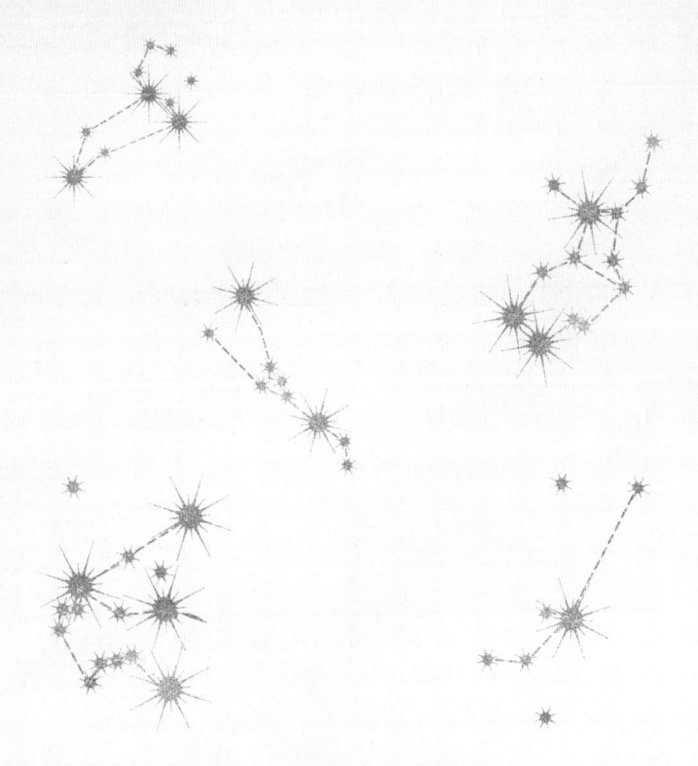

ASTROLOGICAL SUN SIGNS OF THE ZODIAC AND FENG SHUI

Just as feng shui values the five natural elements of wood, earth, fire, metal, and water—with their vital characteristics to enhance and harmonize our homes and lives—Nature's four key elements as revered by Western philosophies—fire, earth, air, and water—are found in the astrological Sun signs of the Zodiac.

When looking at the characteristics of each zodiac sign, consider how best to manage and harmonize your home, family, and friends having an off day, or how to teach and encourage values in your children, or simply laugh more to make it all worthwhile. With knowledge, you can work to utilize the positive and minimize the negative.

Tending the magical fires of love, family, and friendship makes them crackle and sparkle even brighter. Keep these earthly elements in mind to nurture and grow with those you love.

FIRE SIGNS

ARIES
(March 21–April 20)
The Ram

LEO
(July 23–August 22)
The Lion

SAGITTARIUS
(November 23–December 21)
The Centaur

Those in your home born under a fire sign are courageous, intelligent, proud, and determined. They light the way for others and provide the spark of change. Be careful, though, because fire is also aggressive, impatient, and destructive. Tend to fire signs gently to keep them from wreaking unnecessary havoc.

EARTH SIGNS

TAURUS
(April 21–May 21)
The Bull

VIRGO
(August 23–September 23)
The Maiden

CAPRICORN
(December 22–January 20)
The Mountain Goat

Just as the Earth grounds us, earth signs are especially disciplined, grounded, steadfast, analytical, practical, and productive. On those not-so-good days, they may also be stubborn, critical, selfish, and just plain no fun. When these seismic shifts occur, it's important to remember that even our steady Earth wobbles occasionally in orbit. So, all will return to normal soon.

AIR SIGNS

GEMINI (May 22–June 21) The Twins	LIBRA (September 24– October 23) The Scales	AQUARIUS (January 21– February 19) The Water-Bearer

Air signs in our family can be the wind beneath our wings. They are friendly, charming, cooperative, generous, and perceptive. The opposite traits exhibited include indecisiveness, inconsistency, and aloofness. Never knowing which way the wind will blow can leave others off-kilter, but air signs freshen everything they touch. So, take a deep breath and relax.

WATER SIGNS

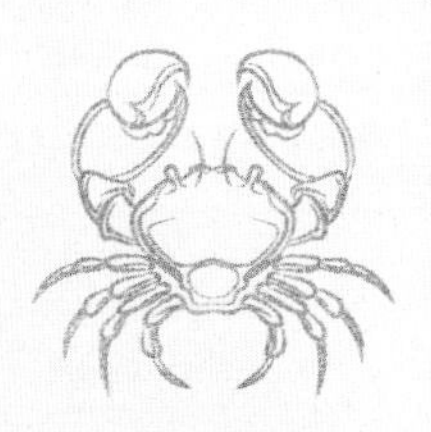		
CANCER (June 22–July 22) The Crab	SCORPIO (October 24– November 22) The Scorpion	PISCES (February 20– March 20) The Fish

Water is life-giving, nurturing, and calming. People born under these signs are dreamers, creative, loyal, and sensitive. They can also be emotional, indecisive, and jealous—traits that can drown even the heartiest of souls. Water signs need security to keep their energies from evaporating.

DECORATE ACCORDING TO YOUR SIGN

Sun's light contains the energy of all colors combined. Shining that light through a prism or crystal bends, or refracts, the individual wavelengths of color to be visible independently, as the Sun's light refracts through water droplets after a rain and enchants us with a rainbow.

As we've seen, colors are energy. They can help set intentions (see page 14), as well as influence mood, confidence, thoughts, and feelings. Each zodiac Sun sign has a specific color that gives voice to its personality and plays up its natural charms—as if the Sun's light shone through the prism of the zodiac at birth and your color was born.

Use the following chart to determine the best colors for you and other family members. Spread them throughout the home for a sense of familial harmony, or use them in an individual's room to highlight their individual personalities. Wear them. Eat them. Use what speaks to you. Have fun with color and the zodiac.

Aries

Color: Red

Purpose: Fill your home with your passion and your life with your energy.

Taurus

Colors: Green, pink

Purpose: Natural elements surrounding you, especially lush green plants, keep you grounded and growing strong.

Gemini

Color: Yellow

Purpose: Brighten your home and the smiles of all those around you with this sunny color.

Cancer

Color: White

Purpose: Surrounding yourself and your home with white is like wrapping up in the wisdom of the Moon's soft light. Boost intuition and let love flow.

Leo

Colors: Gold, orange

Purpose: The richness of gold promotes generosity—of time, money, spirit, patience, and love.

Virgo

Color: Beige

Purpose: A symbol of Earth, beige allows growth and provides stability to support it.

Libra

Colors: Light blue, light pink

Purpose: Blue is calm and cool, just like Libra's sense of fairness, and because of your fairness, you're liked by all; pink vibrates with friendship.

Scorpio

Colors: Shades of deep red

Purpose: These colors ignite passion and your desire to get to the heart of the matter; look beneath the surface for true meaning.

Sagittarius

Colors: Dark blue, purple

Purpose: Colors of royalty and abundance. Tap into your natural positivity and await new opportunities.

Capricorn

Colors: Black, brown

Purpose: Solid, reliable, and traditional. Your natural determination is supported.

Aquarius

Colors: Light blue, silver

Purpose: Calming waters for a restless soul.

Pisces

Colors: Aquamarine, sea green

Purpose: Colors of life and growth. Reflections of the sea encourage the dreamer within.

YIN-YANG SYMBOL

This deeply philosophical symbol with its origins in ancient Taoist philosophy represents the contrast and confluence of the *yin*—dark, cold, hard, feminine, passive—and the *yang*—light, warm, soft, masculine, active—forces in all things. One cannot exist without the other and the interactions of the two create the five elements: wood, fire, earth, metal, and water.

By living in harmony with Nature and our surroundings, in all aspects of our life, we come to realize that life is not black or white, good or bad, but it is black *and* white, good *and* bad. When we can accept and understand this disconnect exists in all things—at once, or at different times—we live with more ease in the constantly shifting, sometimes confusing, world we call home.

THE MAGIC OF EARTH
GREENERY, BLOOMS, AND ESSENTIAL OILS

May the spirit of Nature abound and uplift every day of the year.

The magnificent Earth—at once grounding, fertile, stable, nurturing, long-lived, yet constantly renewing—is believed to hold magical powers that can heal and transform our lives in many ways and that can be invoked to support the stability and healthy abundance of our homes, lives, and families. Emanating from her energetic core and the individual energies of her abundant flora and fauna, the Earth offers immense gifts on a daily basis.

The Earth sustains life and her energy brings growth. By working with her and connecting to her power, we will bring positive energy into our lives that will keep our homes in peace and calm. From herbs and flowers to essential oils, Nature can offer us transformative energy. Tap into these natural gifts to bring harmony to your home and enhance your spiritual work.

To begin exploring Earth's energy and seeking her healing wisdom, try simple meditation. Start slowly and build your routine as you become greater acquainted with absorbing the Earth's energy and receiving her messages. You'll be surprised at what positive things the Earth brings into your home.

EARTH'S HEALING MEDITATION

The Earth's energies can heal physically, emotionally, and spiritually. Her messages may be subtle or powerful. As with all things, be open to those messages and flexible in their interpretations.

Take a few moments to meditate, being present with the Earth. Listen to her heartbeat and let her intuitive prompts draw out your purpose. Feel her restorative energy fill you with strength.

Prepare. Sit comfortably outside, in a quiet location where you can physically connect with the Earth. If that is not possible, sit comfortably in your favorite room and hold an Earth-born object, such as a crystal, stone, or flower.

Observe. Using all your senses, notice as much of your surroundings as you can. Taste: bring fresh water with you, or savor fresh fruit or vegetables from the garden. Is the water cool? Is the grass warm? Are the leaves whispering? Can you smell the waves? What visual captures your imagination?

Focus. Close your eyes and focus on your breathing. In. Out. Slowly. Fully. With each breath in, imagine the Earth's energy filling you up, up, up to the top of your head. With each breath out, see your energy flowing back into the Earth, connecting you as one. Continue to breathe as long as you need.

State your intention. When you feel connected to Earth, state your intention to Earth and be open to her response. Your intuition may become fully engaged. You may feel physical energy—in your body, in the movement of the wind, in the touch of the Sun's warmth. You may receive a message from Nature. You may feel nothing and will have to wait until next time, *or maybe the message is in the delay.*

When you are ready, open your eyes and bring your attention to your physical surroundings, knowing that whatever message you received, or did not receive, you will feel renewed with your connection to the natural world.

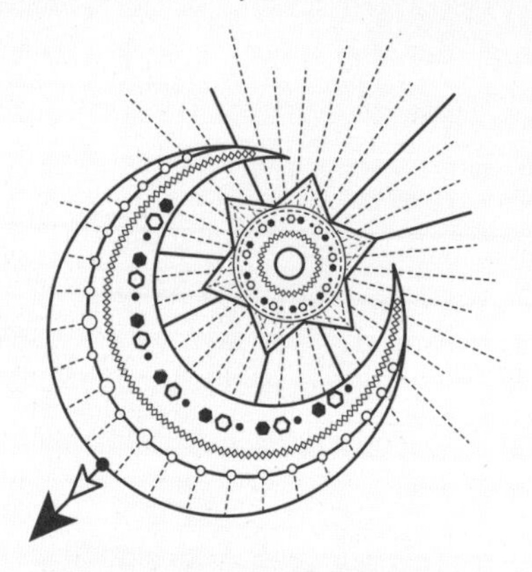

GUIDING SEASONS

Here we will consider the effects of the seasons and look at how to work with the energies of Earth's offerings, such as plants, herbs, and flowers, to enhance our homes and our lives. Earth undeniably brings its unique magic to our lives.

Consider the quiet stillness of winter—its innate sense of rest and replenishment. Plants and animals seek shelter for winter's long slumber. Humans gather indoors as the day's light diminishes and temperatures dictate.

Spring follows winter with its burst of joyful color and scents that awaken the senses and stirs hope and activity. Green, the color of luck and Nature, is on display everywhere. The scent of spring's first roses transports us outside.

Spring ripens to summer. Abundance is everywhere and energies are high. Sunlight bathes us in its healing rays, for long lazy days and sweet soulful nights. The lazy bees' buzz or cicadas' cantata is background music to our lives.

Summer changes her wardrobe to autumn's brilliant hues, but days again grow shorter and a crispness in the air signals winter's return.

Whether you live on a property with bountiful land, in a city dwelling with only a windowsill, or somewhere in between, connecting with Nature and all she has to offer has been shown to reduce stress, invite creativity, heal, and lift the spirits.

Borrow a tip from Nature's generous charm book for inspiration in your home and life. Heed her messages and seek her wisdom to harvest the best from every day for the purposeful life you envision.

GREENERY

Create a Nature conservancy in your home, or select a single beautiful plant to brighten and purify one room. Whatever your goals, the simplest way to invite Nature in is by adding houseplants to your environment. Not only do they beautify your space, but they also offer health benefits, including cleaner air, reduced allergens, healing abilities, and nutritional boosts. Consider these suggestions, which include some easy plants and some more finicky options—just like tending relationships with family, coworkers, and friends.

AFRICAN VIOLET

Care: Grows well in indirect and artificial light; prefers lukewarm water, feed from the bottom

Magical uses: Purple color can brighten mood and help you relax; favored for its nod to spirituality and powers of protection, especially for the home.

Suggested rooms: Family room, living room

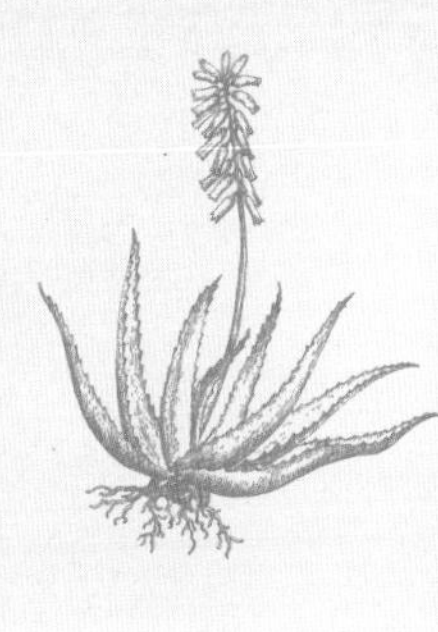

ALOE VERA

Care: Needs only occasional watering but significant sunlight to grow

Magical uses: This plant's healing qualities have been revered for years, and growing one is said to prevent accidents in the home. The leaves' gel can ease the sting of burns and bug bites, and may offer digestive relief. It promotes patience and has a reputation for enhancing beauty.

Suggested rooms: Kitchen

BOSTON FERN

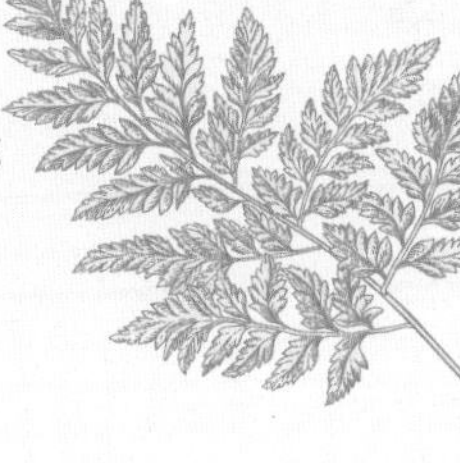

Care: Likes direct sun; benefits from a regular misting

Magical uses: Purifies and adds humidity to the air, which can help dry skin.

Suggested rooms: Bathroom, porch, office

CACTI

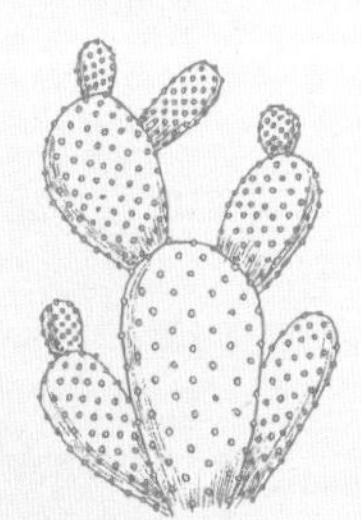

Care: Love dry, warm, sunny conditions; great for beginners

Magical uses: Beauty in all shapes and sizes; add visual interest and help purify the air; slow growers offer lessons in patience. Look to cactus for protection.

Suggested rooms: Entry, living room, office

FRESH FLOWERS

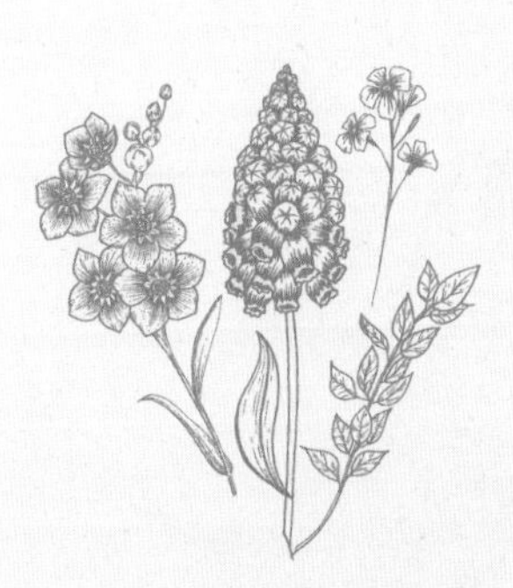

Care: Trim the stems, add to a vase, fill with water . . . instant joy

Magical uses: Enhance mood with their beauty, color, and scent.

Suggested rooms: Any room

ORCHID

Care: Occasional watering; likes humidity; bright light is best; can be higher maintenance

Magical uses: Blooms instantly uplift and are said to lend positive energy to a space; increases concentration and willpower

Suggested rooms: Family room, living room, office, sunroom

PEACE LILY

Care: Will thrive in partial sunlight; likes a humid environment

Magical uses: Purifies the air; often used as a symbol of sympathy, conveying a spiritual meaning to many.

Suggested rooms: Bathroom, dining room, kitchen

VARIEGATED SNAKE PLANT

Care: Likes low light; can tolerate infrequent watering

Magical uses: Purifies the air and may increase luck.

Suggested rooms: Entry, family room, kitchen, study

Note: As with all things you bring into your home, research the safety of these plants for your animal friends, if they live there, too.

FLAVOR LIFE WITH AN HERB GARDEN

Another simple way to bring Nature's magic into your home is by tapping into the miracles that are fresh herbs. They add flavor to food, scents to bouquets, magic to intentions, and substance to spellwork. Tuck them into a wreath, based on intentions set, or sprinkle them in food to tend to your family's well-being.

Growing herbs typically requires access to the Sun's magical rays and soothing water to encourage their growth; they can be easily nurtured outdoors directly in a garden, in a pot on your patio, or set on a sunny windowsill—inside or out. A few tools and you'll be cultivating your own herbal magic in no time. No garden? Purchase fresh herbs from your grocer or local farmers' market. Remember, organic is best.

Following is a guide to some culinary herbs and their meanings. Use these herbs as they correspond to your intentions, or include them in spellwork to entice what you desire.

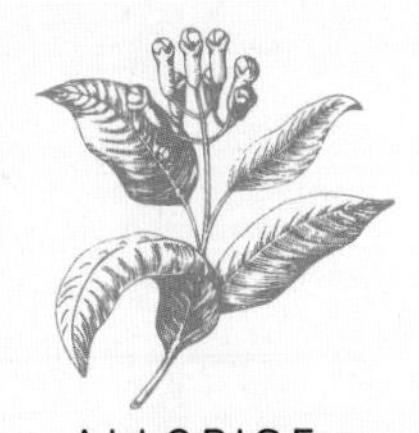

ALLSPICE

energy, healing, luck, virility

CARDAMOM

aphrodisiac to some, charm, relaxation

BASIL

courage, good wishes, love, wealth

CHAMOMILE

comfort, patience, sleep

BAY LEAF

glory, strength, success

CHIVES

utility

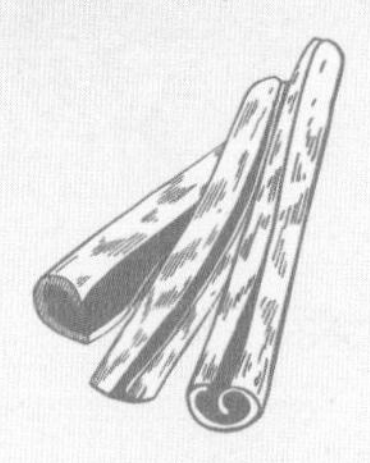

CINNAMON

abundance, connection to the spirits

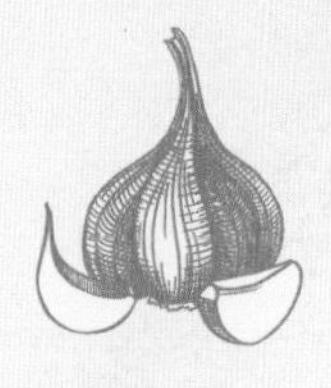

GARLIC

aphrodisiac, passion, strength
(and repelling the odd vampire or two)

DILL

luck, protection from evil

LAVENDER

devotion, peace

ECHINACEA

inner strength

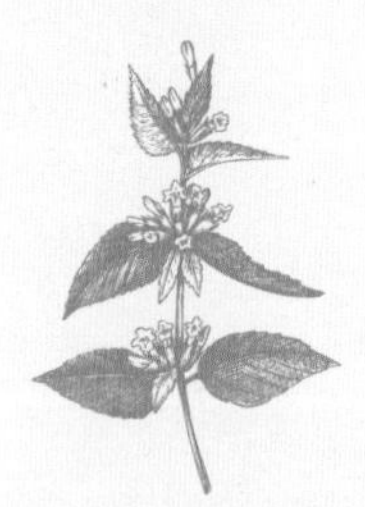

LEMON BALM

sympathy

FENNEL

flattery, praiseworthy

MINT

increases the power of our words,
refreshment, travel

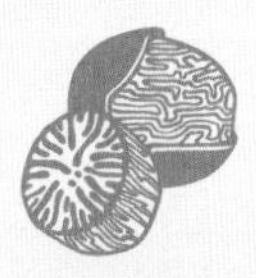

NUTMEG

enhances intuition, increases wealth, lucky charm for games of chance (use whole), travel

SAFFRON

aphrodisiac, mood booster, uniqueness, wealth

OREGANO

add to love potions, grow to protect home from evil influences, tranquility, vitality

SAGE

longevity, wisdom

PARSLEY

celebration, gratitude

THYME

courage

ROSEMARY

clarity, remembrance

YARROW

healing

GARLIC: THE MAGIC PROTECTOR

Garlic can work its magic in almost every room of the home.

Entry: Hanging a garlic braid here can deter thieves—and vampires—from entering your home—as well as the plague. Or, rub your windowsills and doorways for the same effect.

Kitchen: Eat it as part of your meal and, at once, be nourished, lower blood pressure and cholesterol, and enjoy its antibiotic properties.

Bedroom: Consume it before bedtime as an aphrodisiac and hang it outside the bedroom door to beckon your suitor. A garlic braid hung in their rooms carries ancient wisdom to protect children from evil.

Bathroom: Inhaling garlic essential oil as part of a steam treatment can clear the sinuses blocked from a cold.

Office: Garlic is said to bring good luck, so eat it with abandon in your home office, or stash some in a drawer to double down; it will up your lucky odds and keep away luck-sucking evil spirits.

THE LANGUAGE OF FLOWERS

In addition to their beauty and delicious scents, flowers speak their own language, one that's easy to learn. Select your bouquet based on your intended recipient or the energy needs in your home. Incorporate some herbs for their special scents and meanings, too (see page 84). Keep flowers well-watered to keep the conversation flowing.

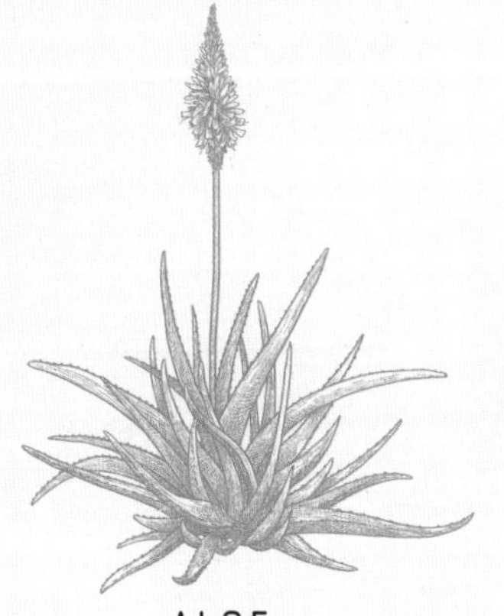

ALOE
grief, healing

BLACK-EYED SUSAN
justice

APPLE BLOSSOM
preference

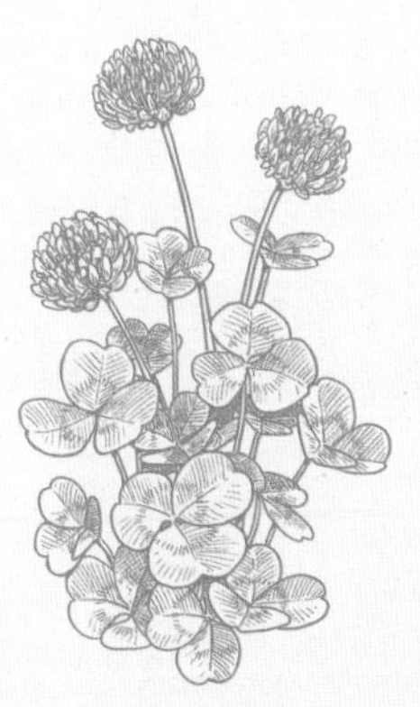

CLOVER
good luck

DAFFODIL

high regard

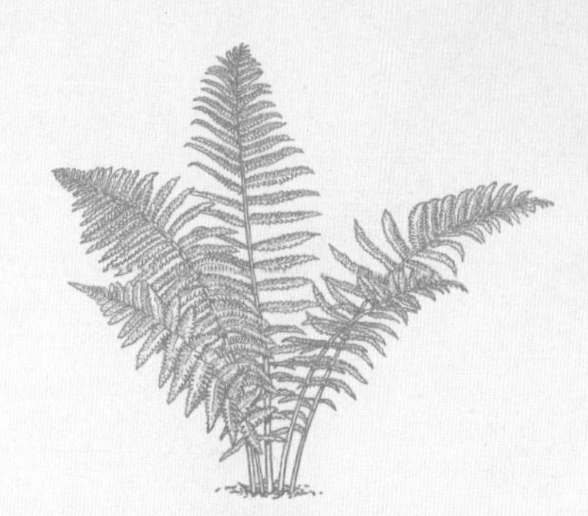

FERN

magic

DAISY

hope

ENGLISH IVY

fidelity

DELPHINIUM

cheerfulness, encouragement, protection

LILAC

sweet youthful joy

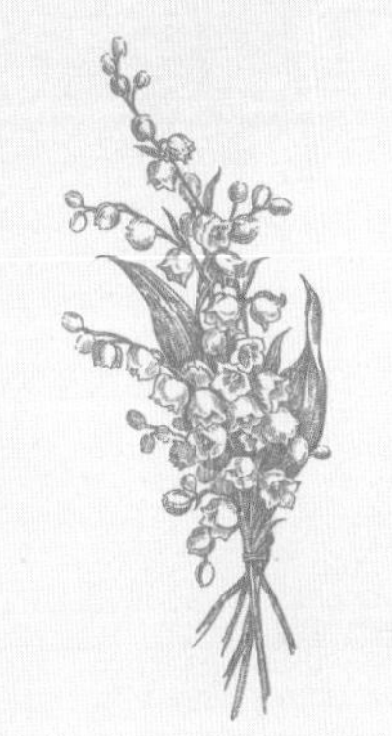

LILY OF THE VALLEY

returning happiness

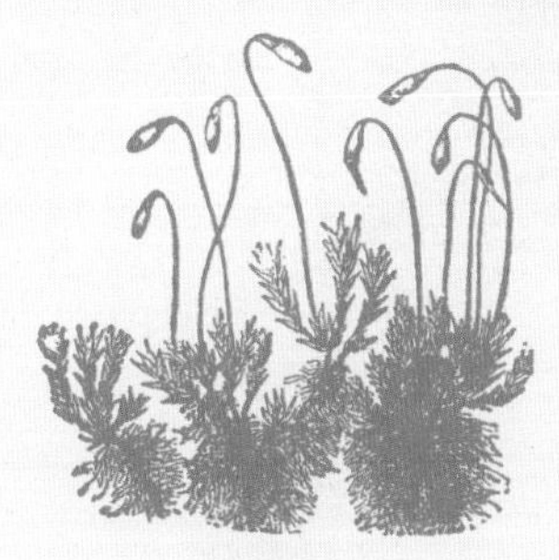

MOSS

maternal love

MARIGOLD

justice, fairness, protection

PANSY

free thought, nostalgia, remembrance

MISTLETOE

surmounting difficulties

PINK CARNATION

lasting memories

PINK ROSE

happy friendship

RED ROSE

love

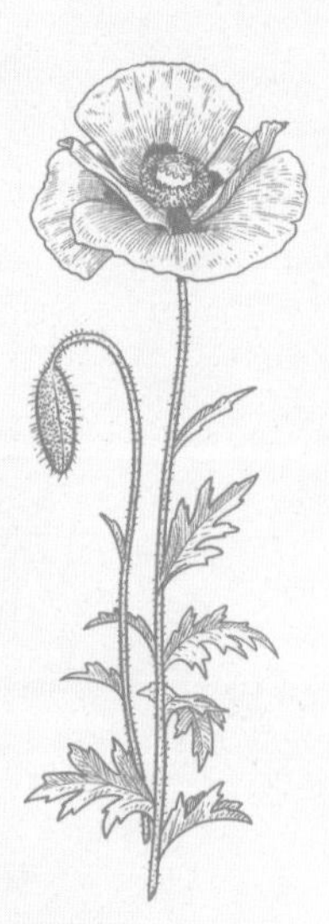

RED POPPY

consolation

RED TULIP

declaration of love and admiration

SNAPDRAGON
protection

VIOLET
devotion, luck

SUNFLOWER
fertility

YELLOW TULIP
smile

Use the language of herbs and flowers not only to advance your intentions and add unique energies to your home, but also to share with friends and family: perhaps a sweet bouquet of clover, basil, or daffodil, with good luck wishes on graduation. Some ideas include the following: healing blooms like yarrow for recovery from illness; comforting chamomile during times of personal loss; or lily of the valley to welcome a loved one home.

FOUR-LEAF CLOVER

A traditional symbol of the Irish on St. Patrick's Day, the three-leaf clover, or shamrock, traces its connection in Irish lore back to St. Patrick in the time of the Druids, when he used the clover to teach the concept of the Holy Trinity as he worked to convert Ireland to Christianity.

The four-leaf clover, though, is revered for its luck. It is said that three of the four petals represent faith, hope, and love—the fourth was added by God for serendipitous good fortune.

So, wear the shamrock to proclaim your lucky status to all. Decorate a room in your home, or your office, with a potted shamrock plant and count the luck of the Irish on your side. You'll also have great good luck keeping kids busy for hours searching the lawn for the four-leaf keepsake!

HERBS AND FLOWERS MAKE A POWERFUL POTION

Whether tucked into a wreath, gathered in a vase, bundled to hang for their scent, or scattered about as you wish, herbs and flowers have powerful natural charms that can help you direct energies and outcomes in your home. Their beauty and scent carry messages of love, luck, fertility, and healing, and they are silent reminders of the intentions you seek to manifest. Try it. You'll see.

Encouragement: delphinium

Family harmony and love: apple blossom, basil, bleeding heart, gardenia, sweet alyssum

Fertility: acorn, carrot, fig, geranium, pine, sunflower

Friendship: lemon, sweet pea

Healing: angelica, bay leaf, fennel, ivy, lemon balm, marigold

Luck and money: basil, bluebell, daffodil, honeysuckle, moss, pine, poppy

New business ventures: bay laurel

New home blessing: myrtle

Protection: cactus, dill, fennel, lilac, peony, rosemary, witch hazel

Remembrance: pansy

Romantic love: carnation, daisy, lavender, lemon verbena, pansy, peppermint, rose, rosemary

Sleep: chamomile, hyacinth, lavender, thyme

Success: bay leaf, jasmine, strawberry

Wisdom: iris, sage, sunflower

As you gather the blooms that will carry your intentions forward, take a moment to thank them for their gifts. For silent they be, but potent you'll see, in lending their ear to your wishes. As you arrange them in whatever fashion you wish, kindly ask for their help, as you need it.

SCENT AND ESSENTIAL OILS

The beauty of flowers and herbs is not limited to their sweet messages. Their transformative powers of scent are just as enticing and have the ability to transport us to another time, another place, and adjust our attitude in the moment. A beautifully scented home is not only pleasing to the nose but can affect the brain as well.

The herbs and flowers that decorate our world contain essential oils, which carry the essence of the plant from which they were extracted, containing all the natural properties and energies of the plant responsible for their variously relaxing, uplifting, mesmerizing, cheery, or energizing scents and effects.

Enjoy the oils' aromatherapy benefits by smelling the oils. Common methods include: diffusing; rubbing the oils onto your body (always done by diluting with a carrier oil, such as sweet almond oil, jojoba oil, or even olive oil); adding to a bath ritual to soothe, energize, calm, or otherwise influence mood; or mixing into creams and lotions for use on the body (with proper precaution, see page 87).

Consider these popular essential oils to conjure a little magic into your everyday life.

BERGAMOT

sweet, floral orange; relieves depressions, freshens and deodorizes, calms and soothes

CEDARWOOD

sweet, cedar closet aroma; improves sleep, boosts energy

CITRUS, SUCH AS ORANGE AND GRAPEFRUIT

fragrant, fruity, zesty; instant sunshine-filled mood lifter, reduces airborne bacteria

GERANIUM

strong floral scent; calming in small quantities

CLARY SAGE

herbaceous, floral, slight fruity; aphrodisiac, reduces anxiety and stress, relaxing

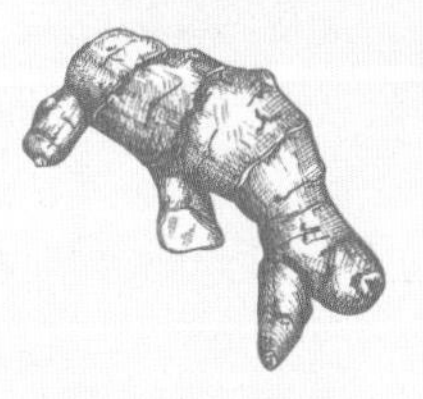

GINGER

warm, spicy, sweet, woody; emotionally and physically warming; instills feelings of confidence, relieves nausea

COMMON SAGE

camphorous, herbaceous; cleansing, eases mental fatigue, improves mood

JASMINE

sweetly floral; promotes feelings of affection, reduces stress and fatigue

EUCALYPTUS

sweet camphorous, slightly mint; clears the mind and energizes the attitude

LAVENDER

floral, herbaceous, slightly camphorous; calms, de-stresses, and relaxes, even promotes sleep

LEMON

bright, fresh, clean, citrusy; energizes, de-stresses, uplifts

PINE

piney, woodsy, Christmas tree; clears the mind and promotes concentration, fosters a positive outlook, reduces stress

LIME

bright, fresh, sweet, citrusy; cheerful, cleanses, purifies, renews the spirit

ROSE

sweetly floral; can calm, heal, and nourish emotions

PATCHOULI

musky, spicy, best described as earthy; aids in meditating and focusing intentions

ROSEMARY

slightly piney, camphorous; clears the mind, energizes, improves memory, invigorating

PEPPERMINT

familiar, minty, menthol; eases aches and pains, energizes, relieves nausea, stimulating, uplifting

SANDALWOOD

sweet, woody aroma; deeply grounding with the ability to instill inner peace

THYME

strongly herbaceous; though known for its antibiotic properties, can also fight off negative vibes and give an instant boost to your mood

YLANG-YLANG

delicate, slightly fruity-floral aroma; boosts creativity, eases stress, and diffuses anger; also acts as an aphrodisiac and relieves depression

CAUTION: PURCHASING, STORING, AND USING ESSENTIAL OILS

Purchase and store. Look for pure oils with no additives. Purchase from brands that practice ethical standards and produce quality products. Store all essential oils out of reach of children and pets.

Use. Do not ingest any essential oil. Some oils can be toxic. Do not use any essential oil on your body undiluted; test a small area for adverse reaction. Do not use essential oils on damaged skin or on young children, pregnant people, pets, or the elderly who may be sensitive to the oils' properties. Consult your health care provider about therapeutic use, which is not recommended here.

INFUSE YOUR HOME WITH THE POWER OF SCENT

Whether to set a mood, magnify intentions, promote peace and meditative opportunities, or infuse healing energies, essential oils are easy to use in your home. Use common sense and follow some precautions (see page 87).

The easiest way to put essential oils to work for you is simply to open the bottle and sniff. Headache coming on? Try a whiff of peppermint essential oil. Big presentation at work? Inhale pine essential oil to reduce stress and focus the mind. Everyday stress tying you in knots? Lavender essential oil can save the day.

Using the same principle, apply a few drops of essential oil to a tissue or cotton ball and place it nearby while at work, or reading, or whenever you need help. The evaporating oil will fill your senses with its energies and ignite your intuition.

DIFFUSERS

Diffusers disperse essential oils into the air to penetrate a larger area for you to inhale their scent and experience the associated benefits. Perhaps use chamomile essential oil in the bedroom to help you relax, or use lemon essential oil in the family room to keep the mood bright. Follow the manufacturer's instructions for the on/off cycle of diffusing, and *be aware of who else may be in the room if caution is needed.*

Personal diffusers also come in the form of jewelry so you can practice self-care when away from home. Some types of jewelry include pads or wicks to which you apply the essential oil. Some necklaces include tiny glass bottles with cork stoppers for you to fill with your favorite oil. Other types of jewelry are made of absorbent materials like clay, porous stones, or rope.

POTPOURRI

Customize a potpourri based on the energies, scents, or messages of the herbs and flowers used. Support your intentions or enhance the purpose of your rooms.

- Welcoming entry
- Energetic family room
- Nurturing kitchen
- Cleansing bath
- Romantic bedroom
- Soothing child's room
- Productive office
- Creative studio

Select the blooms based on your intentions—use one type or fragrance or a symphony of scents, colors, and shapes. Separate any herb leaves or flower heads and spread them on newspaper. Set them in an undisturbed, warm, dry location to dry (a few days to a few weeks). You may even want to add spices, like cinnamon sticks or peppercorns, or dried fruits, like citrus slices. Make sure everything is fully dried before proceeding.

Transfer the dried potpourri to a wide-mouth glass jar with a tight-fitting lid, or individual sachet bags. Select an essential oil to boost the dominant scent, or complement it, and add a few drops. Cover the jar and let sit for a few days before opening and releasing its spirit into the room.

If you chose sachets, tuck them into drawers, hang them from doorknobs or in closets, or position them on bookshelves around the room. When the scent starts to fade, refresh it with a few drops of essential oil.

Your home is your haven, and your intentions guide your life, your family, your joy. Let Nature help you manifest all your dreams to the highest power.

BIRDS: SYMBOLIC CURRIERS

Birds are a daily presence, even living in our homes as pets, and they are astounding creatures. They fly high above Earth across neighborhoods, oceans, and continents! Many birds, such as eagles, hawks, herons, and falcons (see Horus, page 35), hold religious and cultural import and are viewed as messengers of good and evil—even representing the gods. Birds frequently also represent eternal life and our flight from an earthly existence to a heavenly one.

These ancient harbingers offer us messages even today, but you must be open to receiving them and aware of their presence and knowing your intentions can help you interpret the messages sent. Birds in our dreams can be interpreted as our goals, hopes, and aspirations as well as joy and freedom. Be thankful for their appearance. They deliver heavenly messages from our guardian angels. It is widely believed the first bird you see after the death of a loved one represents that person returning to you, offering signs of support, protection, and encouragement.

If you want to attract more birds into your home, consider adding bird feeders to your backyard. Bird feeders and foods like peanuts, fruit, and mealworms will welcome a variety of birds to your space. Other ways to attract more birds to your yard or garden include making bird baths, adding moving water like dripping water features, incorporating roost boxes, and nurturing nature with more trees, seed-producing plants, flowers, and shrubs. Birds also love bright colors, so add some bright colors to your garden with colorful flowers.

A bird flying into your home is a sure sign of good luck.

Birds you may see, encounter repeatedly in other ways, or have a natural affinity for, may be telling you this:

BLUE JAY
embodies strength and independence.

CARDINAL
represents a spiritual visit from a deceased loved one.

BLUEBIRD
portends happiness and good luck.

DOVE
illustrates peace and love, especially in pairs.

EAGLE

symbolizes healing and enlightenment.

HAWK

encourages observing the larger perspective—specifically one's spirit self and power.

GOOSE

demonstrates faithfulness in the face of hardships.

HERON

a reminder to practice patience.

HUMMINGBIRD

spreads joy, hope, and love.

MOCKINGBIRD

though he imitates, he can help you find your true voice and higher purpose. He also speaks of courage and innocence.

OWL

lends intuition, wisdom, and is the messenger of news.

PIGEON

signifies home and security.

ROBIN

sings of good luck.

RAVEN

symbolic of death, not necessarily physical, but the end of something significant. Alternatively, as far back as Viking times, the raven was venerated by sailors for its uncanny ability to locate land, so perhaps it offers guidance as well.

ROOSTER

announces a new day, new beginnings, and represents our spirituality.

SPARROW

may appear mundane, but pushes us to take a closer look closer and observe the significance and importance of every day.

SWALLOW

tells of spring's blossoming.

STORK

delivers change, good luck, and fertility.

SWAN

reflects elegant beauty and grace.

THE MAGICAL ENERGY OF WATER AND CRYSTALS

May love and happiness flow freely in this home.

Crystals and water may, at first, seem unrelated. There are many similarities and overlap in energies, but the most magical is the shared beauty of the rainbow. Whether conjured from the simple interaction of light and water, or crystal and light, or observed in the spectrum of dazzling colors the crystals display, the visuals are breathtaking and the vibrational energy is intense.

The sea's siren call. The thrill of the ocean's pounding surf. The push and pull of the tides. Ripples in a pond. The soothing feel of immersing oneself fully in water. The attraction is hard to deny. The human body is composed of nearly 60 percent water, meaning we need it to live and we find ourselves drawn to it as a similar creature. Humans also come from the Earth as do crystals.

When crystals formed deep within the Earth are revealed to us, they bear stories of connection. They grow from water rich in dissolved minerals, melted rock, and even vapor. Time, temperature, and pressure shift and mold them into dazzlingly beautiful colors and forms.

Here we'll look more in depth at two of Earth's ancient elements and consider how to utilize their gifts and wisdom in our lives and homes to manifest our dreams and desires.

WATER

Born of the heavens but nurtured by Earth, water is one of Nature's most powerful elements. At home, water soothes, heals, cleanses, hydrates, feeds, nurtures, mystifies, clarifies, supports, and incubates—and facilitates travel to explore the world away from home.

Water is our feminine goddess, the Moon, intuition, emotion, and fluidity.

Water is liquid, solid, gas.

Water is divine.

Be thankful for the easy access to water in your life. There is no end to the way water can create magic in our homes.

Whole house: Clean with intention. Your living space is sacred. It should be clean, uncluttered, and full of positive energy. So, next time it's not, clean with intention. Clear the clutter—clear the negative energy in the room. Clear the dust—clear the cobwebs tangling your thoughts. Clean the windows—let the energizing Sun fill the house with its rejuvenating rays. Sweep the floor—kick the bad mood to the curb.

Kitchen: Cook and drink with a grateful heart. Give a short nod of gratitude to the water you drink or boil food in.

Bathroom: Take a cleansing soak (see Scented Salt Soak, page 124), or establish a meditation ritual bath for renewal.

Garden and porch: Water the flowers and meditate on each individual plant's beauty and fragrance. Breathe in the scents and breathe out any worry or negativity from the day.

Yard, bathroom, kitchen: A child's giggles echo happiness into eternity. Look for ways to engage your kids in joyful play with water. Sprint through a sprinkler. Splash in a pool. Stomp in a puddle. Float a flotilla in the tub. Build a snowman. Run through the raindrops. Eat a snow cone on a hot day.

Bedroom: Meditate with the rain or falling snow.

Living room: Release anger and fear in a thunderstorm.

Family room: Look for a rainbow and make a wish.

Kitchen or bathroom: Wash a friend or relative's hair who may be sick or unable. The soothing water and gentle human touch will be a gift to you both.

If you look deeply enough into a pool of water, it's said you can see into your soul.

SCRYING

Scrying is the act of divination, a process by which one seeks to foretell the future. It has been practiced for thousands of years. Among the many tools used to gain insight into future events are the oft-gazed crystal ball and other reflective objects such as mirrors, polished stones, candle flames, and water—Earth's natural reflector.

If you're lucky enough to live by a natural body of water, use its powers. Sit by it, as the ancients did, and observe its natural ebb and flow to divine your messages. Doing so under the gaze of the full moon invites the goddess Moon and goddess Earth to join you.

As in meditation, where you strive to focus the mind on your breathing or a particular sound to provide the unconscious room to work, the same principle is at work here. Select a quiet time when you have time to spend and will not be disturbed.

- Find a plain, deep, smooth bowl of any size, preferably made of a natural material like glass, stone, or wood. Fill it with water—water charged by the energies of the Sun or Full Moon lends more energy to the experience. Keep any extra water for sipping or tea. Perhaps add a drop or two of essential oil that corresponds with what's on your mind.
- Place the bowl somewhere you can sit comfortably and look into the surface of the water—someplace quiet with soft lighting is ideal.
- Take a minute to center yourself and focus on the problem or intention before you. Breathe and relax.
- Focus your gaze on the water. Let your gaze soften. Focus your mind on the water and let it stay clear. If your mind wanders, acknowledge it and return your focus to the water.
- Continue to gaze into the water, keeping a clear mind. Images may come to you, or your intuition may speak. Tapping deep into the well of your unconscious takes practice. Don't be discouraged if you're unsure of the results immediately.

The answers are wisely within you . . . the water gently reflects what's in your heart so you may see its messages more clearly.

SOOTHING MAGIC

The spiritually soothing ritual of a cup of tea is observed in many cultures. In addition to the bodily nourishment it provides, it can nurture mind and soul. Simply holding the warm cup in your hands and inhaling the soothing aroma can provide an instant feeling of well-being.

Herbs and tea leaves carry with them the energies derived from the Earth in which they were grown, the water that nurtured them, and the unique vibrational energies and healing properties in their natural essential oils. When combined with the healing, soothing properties of water, a cup of tea is Nature's balm to a number of household issues. And, with so many herbal tea blends on the market, each created for its own specific purpose, there is no excuse not to take a me-time teatime break—sit back, sip, and savor.

Whether you choose to purchase your herbal tea or use fresh herbs from your gratitude garden, select a single herb or blend based on intention. As you steep your tea, close your eyes and inhale the aromas while you take time to meditate, even if for just a few seconds, on your intentions. Sweeten with dried fruits, spices, or honey, as desired. All outcomes must be for the good, or your tea will be used in vain.

- Need a boost of motivation to complete a difficult task at home? Try rosemary, peppermint, cinnamon, or a blend.
- Homework, cooking, cleaning, and extracurricular schedules have you coming and going all at once? Call a time-out with lemon balm, rose tea, or a blend with hibiscus.
- Need to unwind from the day and find some inner calm? Drink chamomile, lavender, or peppermint tea, or a blend made to soothe stress.
- Tackling a weighty problem? Put your dreams and intuition to work with the help of rose, cinnamon, and bay leaf.
- Need a rendezvous with romance? Rose, lavender, jasmine, rooibos, strawberry, and chai can all help answer the call.
- If grief or sadness is holding you back, some much-deserved self-care can include a cup of holy basil and rose hip tea and a talk with a friend.

BREWING MAGIC

To make the perfect cup of tea, whether you choose to purchase dried or fresh herbs, or use herbs you've grown in your garden, *always use organic for their purity.*

A general formula is 2 to 3 teaspoons of dried herbs (weight varies) for each 8 ounces (240 ml) of boiling water. For larger quantities, say a 1-gallon (3.8 L) jar, start with about 1 cup (weight varies) of dried herbs.

If you prefer fresh herbs, toss a large handful, or more as desired, into a teapot. Cover the herbs with boiling water and let steep for at least 5 minutes, or longer as desired. Close your eyes and inhale the aromas while you take the time to meditate, even if for just a few seconds, on your intentions. Sweeten with dried fruits, spices, or honey, as desired.

CRYSTALS

Each crystal vibrates with a unique energy and bears the vibrations of the Earth, Moon, Sun, and oceans from which it was born. When you connect with the individual energies of crystals to bring their magical influence into your home, you can create a happier place, one that feels safe, secure, peaceful, creative, and supportive. Focusing your energies and intentions on crystals and strategically placing them throughout your home will align their energies with your priorities—and their very presence reminds you of what's important in your world.

CHOOSING CRYSTALS

Crystals come in a multitude of types, shapes, colors, sizes, uses, vibrational energies, and prices, which means choosing which crystals to bring into your home is a personal decision. Take time to research crystals based on your circumstance, needs, and their source. Start with one that speaks strongly to you—whether through its beauty, sentimental value, vibrational energy, or abilities—and build a personal treasure chest slowly.

Any crystal you choose to add to your home can offer a vibrational boost of healing energy. You can't choose wrong. Trust your gut. That is your intuition at work, recognizing what you need even if you're unsure.

CRYSTAL ENERGIES

The natural vibrations emanating from crystals are believed by some to promote healing, acting as a gateway to both disperse negative energy and allow positive energy to flow in to replace it. When you invite crystals into your life, do so with an open and receptive mind and heart and the power of your intentions. They will respond in kind.

When first bringing crystals home, or after working with them for a while, you will want to reset them to clear any negative energy they may contain and rebalance their vibrational energies. There is no rule for when to do this. Consider cleansing your crystals if they are in a room where someone has been ill or an argument has taken place, or when handled by others who may have disrupted their natural energy. The more you use your crystals, the more in tune you will be with when a recharging is in order.

If the crystal is water resistant, a simple dip in a cool water bath can be enough to cleanse it. Add a pinch of Himalayan salt (see page 110) for a cleansing boost, if desired. If a crystal is not water resistant, leave it in the Moon's cleansing light for a few hours and it'll be ready to absorb your intentions. See Cleansing, Charging, and Recharging Objects with Enchanting Energy (page 120) for how the Moon and Earth may be of additional assistance in maintaining your crystals.

While you can also cleanse crystals in the Sun's magical light, it can fade many crystals, so do some research before using the Sun to reset your crystals.

When not in use, your hardworking crystals still deserve your care and protection. Keep them in a safe place to prevent damage or dust collection.

EXPLORING CRYSTALS FOR A HAPPY HOME

Using and displaying crystals in your home, or wearing or carrying them for adornment, can be for purely decorative reasons. Using them purposefully, however, based on their individual energies and your intentions and needs, can enhance your living space and influence the vibrations of all who live there as well.

Place crystals strategically in a room based on feng shui principles (see page 50), or not so strategically based on what you think looks and feels good. Wear them, carry them in a pocket or pouch, keep them nearby (such as under a pillow, on your desk, or in a wallet), or incorporate them into your day any other number of ways you can think of.

Crystals represent another option to bring Nature indoors, offering beauty, protection, and spiritual, emotional, and physical healing; they can amplify your intention work, assist in meditation, send and receive messages from spirit guides, and deepen natural intuition channels.

As with all things magical, there is no right or wrong way to use or select crystals. Some suggestions follow for crystals particularly beneficial to home life, but use what you have, what you like, or what speaks to you most strongly. *The crystals can choose you* based on the energy vibrations you're sending out as easily as you can choose the crystal.

Amethyst

This royal purple stone is thought to protect you from drunkenness—should you keep one on you while imbibing—and to protect travelers. It is able to calm emotions and brings on sweet dreams. Amulets carved of amethyst are believed to protect people and property from harm.

Set amethyst around your living space, where it will provide spiritual protection and imbue a calming aura.

Angel Aura Crystal

This clear quartz crystal is bonded with platinum. It is a protective crystal but with a soothing vibration. Used in meditation, it is thought to connect someone with their spirit guide. It can promote loving communication with all those in your life.

Place angel aura quartz in various rooms throughout your home, in groups if you can; it exudes a sweet, loving energy.

Black Tourmaline

Black tourmaline is one of the most powerful protection stones. It forms a shield of sorts, blocking negative and harmful energies and reflecting them back to their source where they belong! Black tourmaline is also a cleansing stone and can help clear negative thoughts, boost self-esteem, and lessen anxiety. It is a strongly grounding stone and can be particularly useful in meditation.

Placed in a single room, such as a child's room or bedroom, black tourmaline radiates a protective shield. Placed at the four corners of your home, or its entryway, it protects against unwanted visitors.

Blue Apatite

Blue apatite is a powerful stone believed to increase motivation in achieving goals. It clears mental confusion and stimulates curiosity. It is an uplifting stone, creating a sense of ease and hopefulness. Blue apatite can stimulate your psychic senses and may offer a conduit to the spirit realm.

Blue apatite is also associated with healthy eating and easing a nervous stomach, so one placed in the kitchen can enhance those energies. Its presence can be a reminder of your goals when it's placed in your office or on an altar.

Blue Lace Agate

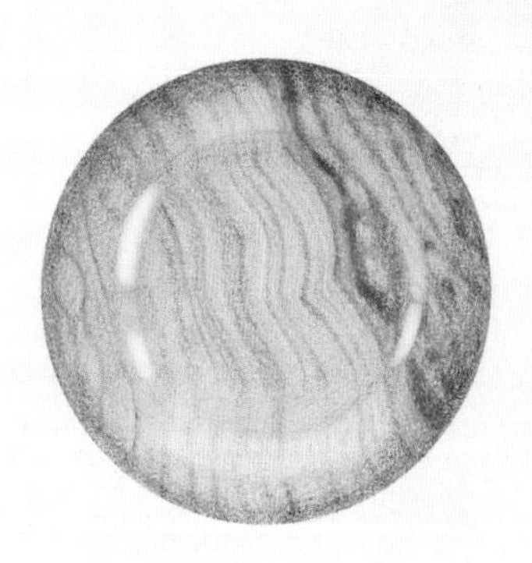

Blue lace agate promotes clear communication, especially under difficult circumstances. Its soothing properties help balance the yin and yang in your universe and promote inner stability.

Placed in the bedroom, blue lace agate can help quiet overactive minds and invite sleep and pleasant dreams.

Celestite

As the name implies, this crystal is a conduit of heavenly communication. Use it in meditation to seek tranquility, divine guidance, or messages from loved ones who have passed. Its soothing energies are a balm for our fears and can aid in healing sadness and grief. Its sky-blue color boosts intuition and the ability to express what we feel.

Place celestite in any room that feels as though it needs an infusion of positive energy. It is especially good in children's rooms to ease fears. In your bedroom, listen for its lullaby from the angels.

Citrine

Citrine radiates sunny optimism. This yellow-hued stone uplifts and bursts with life. Citrine can help clarify your thoughts, especially when seeking new paths. It is a restful stone and good to keep nearby when concentration is required. Citrine manifests abundance and, in turn, increases generosity—sharing wealth brings wealth.

Placed in the center of the home, such as a kitchen or family room, citrine spreads optimism, cheerfulness, and energy throughout.

Clear Quartz

Clear quartz does it all and can take anything you send its way. It is believed to be a master healer and, among other things, encourages positive thoughts, enhances energy, and nurtures patience. Be specific in your intentions when working with clear quartz because it will absorb them fully and amplify them into the Universe. Be sure to listen to the energy vibes sent out in return—they are intended to facilitate personal growth.

Place clear quartz in gathering areas, such as living rooms, family rooms, and porches, to manage the energies colliding from multiple personalities. Add clear quartz to bathwater for an energy-boosting soak.

Garnet

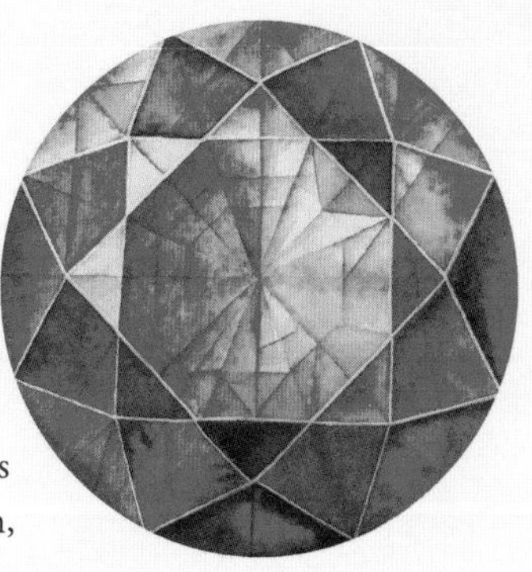

Whatever your passion—in the bedroom or otherwise—garnet can foster the courage to pursue it. This ancient crystal ignites intense feelings and can lift you out of your comfort zone. Its burning color is an outward symbol of this stone's association with love and passion. It is believed to bring luck and has been worn for centuries as a protective talisman. If travel is your passion, carry garnet along for a guide.

Place garnet anywhere you want the energies of warmth and protection. It is especially powerful in the bedroom, but it should be used sparingly.

Green Jasper

This storied stone has a reputation as the "rain bringer." In addition to this valuable quality, it precipitates a myriad of benefits for your crystal toolbox. From easing childbirth to quitting obsessive bad habits, warding off evil spirits, boosting self-control, or dispelling bad dreams, this stone has been revered as sacred and powerful for centuries by diverse civilizations. It is a grounding stone that can stir inner calm at the start of meditation. Its energies can also be absorbed while enjoying a relaxing soak in the tub.

Place green jasper in a child's room for protection. The nourishing aspect of this "rain bringer" makes this stone at home in the kitchen or dining room, and any areas where family gathers.

Himalayan Salt

Himalayan salt, an edible crystal, contains more than eighty trace elements and minerals our bodies need. Its vibrational properties are similar to rose quartz, making it a strong supporter of love—especially self-love. Salt has been used for centuries for energy purification and protection, especially within the home. Its energies are extremely grounding, and its presence in the home is said to invite wealth and abundance.

Place a Himalayan salt lamp in any room to help purify the air, or add a lovely soft, relaxing light to your meditation space or bedroom, where it can help induce sleep (avoid humid locations, as water is not a friend). Add some Himalayan salt to a hot bath, place some on your altar (see page 20), sprinkle it on windowsills to bid evil adieu, or try it in Sage Cleansing Spray (see page 118) to clear the air.

Labradorite

This beautiful multihued stone is believed by the Inuit to have fallen to Earth from the aurora borealis. As such, it brings powers to increase clairvoyance, and its energies will surround you in a magical cloak of protection. It is the stone of new beginnings and limitless potential. Labradorite discourages antisocial behavior and encourages courtesy and friendliness.

Place labradorite in the areas of your home where feeling safe and secure is important, such as a bedroom or any room with a door to the outside.

Malachite

Note: If working with malachite, handle it only in its polished, finished form.

It is the healing deep green color of Nature and offers all the energies to be found there when you seek refuge from material matters. Working with malachite allows our subconscious to reveal what we need and grasp what our emotions are trying to tell us. It instills leadership and the confidence to take action for change and affords protection to loved ones.

Keep malachite in a home study, office, or bedroom as well as on your altar *(see page 20)* *for use in meditation and grounding.*

Rose Quartz

Rose quartz is a nurturing stone offered by Mother Earth as her expression of unconditional love, which includes compassion and forgiveness. Its energies can help heal emotional trauma, ease anxiety, release jealously, mend a forsaken heart, and clear away anything negative that prevents the sending or receiving of love.

Keep rose quartz all around your home to influence loving relationships and healing within your family. As rose quartz equals love of all kinds, cooking is true love, so having one in the kitchen at all times is recommended. In the bedroom, rose quartz can enhance romance and build trust. For adults and children, it can help ease you into sleep and deliver beautiful dreams. Placed on an altar dedicated to romantic love, it can help attract your desires.

Sapphire

This stunning blue crystal is one of hope, wisdom, royalty, and power, reputed to invite happiness, peace, and prosperity into your world. It is a symbol of love and faithfulness. Its energies can help focus the mind, especially when navigating change, as well as expand your ability to see beauty and interpret your intuition.

Use anywhere in the home you want to establish a haven of calm reflection.

Selenite

This stone, whose name means "moon" in Greek, embodies the Moon goddess qualities of blessings, love, and light. Selenite is often used when reaching for spiritual guidance or help from a guardian angel. It can also put you in touch with your own inner wisdom. Its ability to channel the Moon's energy is useful for cleansing and purifying and promotes honest communication.

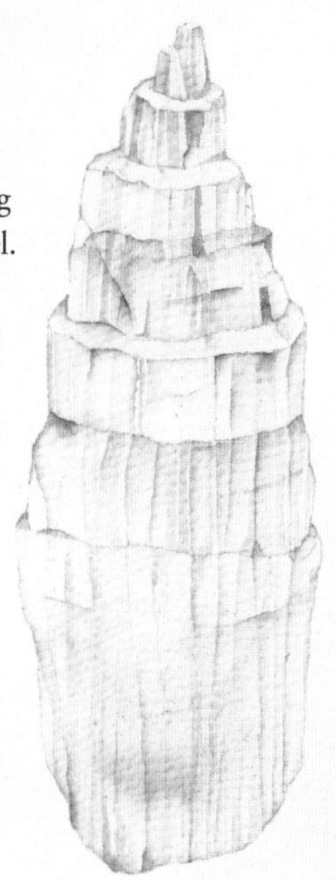

Place selenite near windows in your home to reflect the Sun's light and brighten the space. Place selenite in any room to reflect the Moon's guiding light, and it will spread her caring, comforting energy. Used in any room of the house, especially placed in corners, it cultivates a peaceful, safe space for family living. Keep safe away from water.

Tiger's Eye

Call on tiger's eye when your personal power reserves feel depleted. It can help relieve fear, anxiety, and self-doubt, whether in matters of love or business. Tiger's eye sees within its realm protection, good luck, and prosperity. Tiger's eye can also harmonize disparate energies to create reason while balancing emotion and helping heal tension in families.

Place tiger's eye in any home-based office for prosperity or in any family living areas to promote stable emotions.

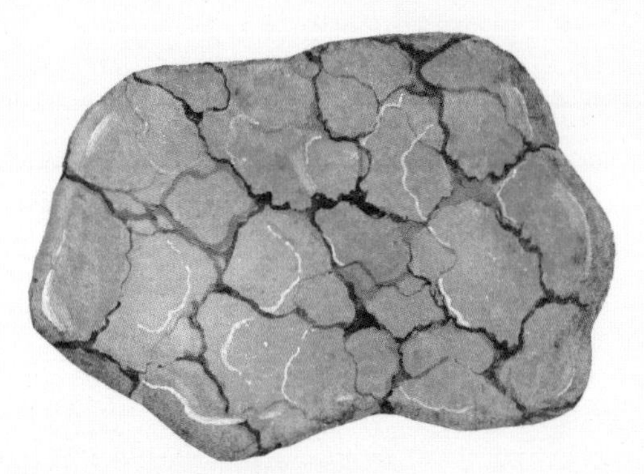

Turquoise

This striking blue-green stone is like holding a piece of heaven. Civilizations across centuries have held this crystal sacred for its powers of wisdom and regal symbolism. Turquoise is said to be a good luck charm, balance emotions, and be spiritually grounding. It promotes serenity, relieves stress, and can remind you of what is important when you listen to your soul—and to see *and accept* all that makes you *you*.

Place turquoise anywhere in your home you seek rest and quiet, such as a bedroom or study.

SPELLS, RITUALS, AND RECIPES TO

CONJURE HOUSE MAGIC

Where Earth, Moon, Sky, and you align—
may each day be kissed with blessings.

Magical living takes place inside and outside the home. I invite you to begin enchanting your world by honoring the energies of the seasons and enlist Nature's inspiring help to manifest your dreams. Let the power of Nature enlighten your path to spiritual growth.

Then, step inside. Each room in your home has its own personality and purpose. Practice a few rituals to keep the magical energy flowing in you and your home as you seek comfort, peace, and that all-healing sleep. Spells by room help you coax the most from each for joyful, loving living. They can be said aloud, spoken silently, or offered as encouragement when needed. They can also be used in rooms other than the ones designated here, as your life and circumstances require.

The rituals and spells outlined in this chapter are meant to get you started. As you get more comfortable and grow your spiritual practice, explore your inner power by creating your own. Use the spells and rituals here to bring more positive energy into your life and living space. Believe in your intentions and in the power of you to make the magic happen—all it takes is a little practice.

HOUSE MAGIC RITUALS

Rituals are organized activities that carry special meaning or mark special occasions. They help bring order to chaos and lend structure that endures. As you strive to keep your home in harmony and balance, look to the natural elements as tools to incorporate into your rituals. Combining the vibrational energies of Nature's gifts creates a symphony that is your life and whose harmonies echo within the walls of your home.

SAGE SMUDGING RITUAL FOR WISDOM AND HEALING PROTECTION

Reset the entire home's energy vibe, or just one room, following the wise lessons of our Native American forebears who honored and sought help and wisdom from the natural elements of the world. Performing a sage smudge cleanses negative energy, darkness, and stagnation, ousts evil spirits, and promotes wisdom and healing in your home.

This simple ritual is powerful in results. You need only basic tools, which are purposeful in their intent to honor the elements, and a willingness to be fully present in the moment. Prepare for a housewarming or house blessing; cleanse a new home or leftover energies in your current home to start the New Year; or refresh your home anytime you feel the energy stagnating, like after an argument or illness.

Gather:

- Dried sage leaves, or a sage smudging bundle, representing **earth**
- 1 heatproof bowl, **water**
- 1 match, **fire**
- Your hand, or a feather, **air**

Close your eyes and visualize clearing the chosen space. Set your intentions for cleansing, protecting, and renewing. Open one or more windows to release trapped energies.

Ancient wisdoms heed my plea that with this wisp of herb all doubts and fear, or anxious tears disperse, float out of sight.
To leave instead a sacred shield to comfort and protect our health and home from life's unknown, or other harmful plight.

1. Place the sage in the bowl. Light it with the match, then carefully extinguish the flame with a wave of your hand.
2. Working in a clockwise direction, which attracts good things to you, encourage the smoke from the smoldering herb out into the room, focusing especially in corners where darkness can hide, so it may absorb what needs to be released.

With burning sage, I walk this path to clear away all smoldering fear and evil that may haunt.

3. When finished, wave the smoke out the window, visualizing it pulling negativity from the room.

Sacred smoke waft doom and gloom afar and out the door. Your scent to stay, keep ills at bay, while life is here abloom.

4. Pause, feel a moment of gratitude for the work done by these herbs and tools.

Caution: Make sure the burning herbs are fully extinguished, such as in water, before returning the ashes to the Earth in a garden, flowerpot, or lawn, if possible, to continue Nature's cycle.

CLEARING NEGATIVE ENERGY: SAGE CLEANSING SPRAY

If burning is not your thing (see Sage Smudging Ritual, page 116), achieve the same results clearing negative energies with a spritz of Sage Cleansing Spray (page 118). It is an easy way to finish intention setting and add a welcoming scent. The spray can also be customized using other essential oils, based on your preference or desired energies. Try a citrus blend for enhancing happiness in rooms such as the kitchen or living room, or a lavender spray to soothe and calm, such as in a bedroom or bathroom.

Gather:

- 8-ounce (240 ml) glass spray bottle (dark glass, if possible)
- Sage essential oil
- ¾ cup (180 ml) distilled water, or Moon- or Sun-infused water (water you've let sit in the Moon or Sun's energizing light for 24 hours) for added vibrational power
- 2 tablespoons (30 ml) vodka or unscented witch hazel
- Himalayan salt

1. Carefully place 8 to 10 drops of sage essential oil (more or less, depending on how strong you like the scent) into a spray bottle.
2. Add ½ cup (120 ml) of water, the vodka (it helps disperse the oil in the water), and a large pinch of salt (to help absorb any negative energies).
3. Add the remaining ¼ cup (60 ml) of water. Cap the bottle and shake to combine, and again before each use.
4. Spray lightly around your space to cleanse the negative energies, avoiding your face and eyes. Opening a window or door to let the energy out is a good idea, if practical. A simple spell can help speed the process:

Sweet sage does banish all that's bad, when energies do sag;
A place of joy is what I seek. No evil can be had.
A spritz, a spray . . . be gone, I say . . . replaced with songs of glad.

HOUSE MAGIC GROUNDING VISUALIZATION

Family, work, school, laundry, housework . . . life . . . can get hectic. When home life doesn't seem quite so charming, or you just need a little self-care to recharge your batteries, this visualization will help you stay in the moment and recapture your focus. It is grounding, uplifting, and energizing all at once.

Earth nurtures me to tend my home to grow my family to change the world. My roots grow strong and deep; my strength runs quiet and clear.

1. Sit comfortably, on the ground or in a chair with your feet flat on the ground, preferably somewhere to feel the Sun's warmth, such as a porch, sunroom, even a family room or kitchen with sunny windows.

2. Close your eyes and focus on your breathing. Breathe in fully, feeling your belly relax and expand. Breathe out slowly, feeling your belly sink. Continue this as long as you like, until you feel relaxed and focused.

3. As you breathe, feel yourself relaxing into your support. Let the Earth support you fully as you sink into her embrace. Imagine roots, from your spine or your feet, growing down into the Earth. Feel them grow deep and strong.

4. As you breathe in, feel the Earth's nourishing energy, minerals, and water flowing up through those roots, into your torso, shoulders, arms, and neck, and out through the top of your head. Feel your limbs growing longer and stronger and up into the sky—perhaps there are leaves sprouting from your fingers.

5. As you breathe in again, imagine the warmth of the Sun traveling down through your head, spine, and roots into the Earth.

6. Imagine the energies from the Sun and Earth combining in your belly, creating a glowing warmth that lights you from within. Sit and enjoy the feeling. See the light glowing from your hair, toes, fingers, and breath.
7. When you feel fully grounded and energized, bring your attention back to your feet or your spine and feel your connection to Earth. Continue to breathe and become aware of your surroundings.
8. When you are ready, open your eyes. Sit for a moment and thank the Sun and Earth for their enrichment and support, feeling refreshed and renewed. State your intentions for the day.

CLEANSING, CHARGING, AND RECHARGING OBJECTS WITH ENCHANTING ENERGY

Crystals and gemstones are the most typical items placed under the Moon's healing touch for clearing, or resetting, their vibrational energy. However, you can infuse everyday household items important to you or critical to your goals with specific intention.

Asking the Moon to imbue your items with her intuition and wisdom can be as simple or elaborate an event as you choose. To start, it's a good idea to cleanse new items, or remove any negative energies they may be carrying with them, before charging or recharging. Simply place the items you wish to cleanse in the Moon's light—outdoors, if safe, on a windowsill receiving the Moon's light, or another area open to the Moon. Cleansing items on first use, or resetting them when you feel the need, has the same purpose: to expel negative energies that may have been encountered and replace them with positive energies to enhance your life.

So, organize the crystals whose energies have diminished for you, lay out your outfit for an upcoming first date or job interview, infuse your yoga mat if you're starting a new practice, or ask the Moon to bless any other items. Leave the item overnight in her presence to be cleansed and charged with positive vibrations.

O' gentle ruler of night skies, your beacon shines so bright—
To heal or guide, or change the tides, in awe, I know your might.
So, here I stand within your glow of gently healing rays,
Do fill these items to the brim with energies both wise and bold,
To guide my thoughts and teach my heart to dance as life unfolds.

The next day, set your intentions for each item, focusing on how you will use it. For example, if you've recharged your favorite crystal, hold it in your hand, close your eyes, and feel the vibrations of the crystal itself and the energies absorbed from the Moon. Hold it near your heart and focus your intentions into it.

Crystal of quartz (citrine, jade, amethyst, etc.), when held so near, do speak to my heart—reveal what's dear. Speak to my hands so actions may reach toward my goals, no doubt or fear.

Other items absorb your intentions the same way, whatever they are. A pitcher of Moon water holds energy to soothe and calm. Use it to make a soothing tea (see page 100), or sip throughout the day for a constant reminder of your goals.

Healing water, slake my thirst for all I do desire. With Moon's bright rays imbued this day, instill me with your fire; each sip, I pray, does show the way toward dreams that do inspire.

A few energized coins may carry the Moon's generosity enough to multiply and share good fortune.

These coins I carry in my purse, though few indeed they be
Remind each day, my riches aren't defined alone by coins that I can see.
Each one of us has wealth to share and gifts to give freely,
These coins in hand, each day I plan, to share with those in need.

INTENTION SETTING RITUAL WITH EARTH'S MAGIC

Just as with the Moon's cleansing energies, you can reset and charge any of your spellbinding objects with the healing and rejuvenating powers of Earth.

Water's cooling, calming, cleansing properties can help remove any negative energies from water-safe items you may use regularly and that need resetting. Water is the most natural ingredient you can use to clean your home. You use it to bathe yourself and your family, and a cold drink of water on a hot summer's day will recharge anyone instantly. Cleanse your water-safe crystals before charging them in the Moon's light for a double burst of spellcasting energy.

The Earth's powerful vibrations can be transmitted to objects you intentionally set out to charge. Focus your thoughts and intentions for the object and place it outside, if safe and you are able, overnight. The Moon and Earth will work together to cleanse, charge, and infuse your object with your best intentions. If it makes sense and is safe, such as with crystals or stones—items that came from the Earth—bury them for enhanced energy transfer.

Carefully plan how you will use these newly energized items for their most powerful good work.

GODDESS RITUAL FOR RENEWAL

Water's flowing energy and life-giving and sustaining properties ensure it is a powerful companion to setting intentions in motion. Life can get dirty. When you feel the need for a relaxing, cleansing bit of self-care, try this ritual bath—you'll be renewed to take care of others.

Brigid, maiden goddess of the hearth (see page 45), is also feted at the first signs of spring, that earthly symbolic time of rebirth and renewal. As such, she is a powerful force to use in meditation, especially during the symbolic cleansing of a renewing ritual bath.

Set your intention for renewal.

Draw a warm bath—or take advantage of any natural body of water nearby for a dip. Light a candle, if you are able—green for Nature's renewal, white for purity and cleansing, or blue for peace and serenity. Let the flame be the beacon that draws in your goddess. Diffuse a relaxing essential oil—whatever you like (see page 84). Slip into the water's healing embrace, relax, and close your eyes.

Soft water soothe and cleanse my soul, my body, heart, and mind.
My sole intent, this moment spent, is to reset, recharge, rewire.
Sweet Brigid, goddess of the spring, please join me in refrain.
Sing fragrant words on whispered breeze to fill my heart with song.

RELAX AND RECHARGE

Infuse your bath with the benefits of essential oils—get energized for the day ahead, or unwind from the day just done. Select the essential oil you use accordingly (see page 84).

In the Bath

Lavender, rose, chamomile, and neroli essential oils are all good bets. Bath time is relaxing time and these oils promote those feelings. ALWAYS dilute essential oils with a carrier oil (jojoba, sweet almond, even olive) and add them to a full tub of warm water: In a small glass bowl, stir together 1 tablespoon (15 ml) carrier oil and 10 to 12 drops of essential oil of choice. Instant spa soak!

Happy Feet

Treat your feet well and they will carry you far in life. Give those tired toes special treatment with a foot soak at the end of a long day and throw in some Epsom salt to soothe. You'll feel renewed and ready to tackle anything the family throws at you.

In the Shower

Apply 10 drops of essential oil to a clean washcloth, sponge, or cotton ball. Place the item on the shower floor or inside edge of the tub out of direct contact with the water. As you shower, inhale the natural energies to empower you.

With soothing water, calming oil, and respite from housework's toil,
This mini soak or hurried shower can dissolve the stress and renew my power.

SCENTED SALT SOAK

Epsom salt has been soothing aches, pains, and sprains for hundreds of years. Though exactly how this works hasn't been proven, our grandmothers and their grandmothers have known for generations what helps their families feel better. Epsom salt can help ease itching, relieve minor arthritis pain, soothe swollen feet, and help ease pulled muscles. Combined with the soothing powers of essential oils, this is a match made in self-care heaven.

Grab a bag of Epsom salt—only a few dollars at your local drugstore—or splurge a little for a bag infused with essential oils to up the relaxation quotient. Or make your own, if you're so inclined.

Note: For bath time, avoid warming essential oils like peppermint, clove, or ginger, as they may irritate the skin.

- 2 cups (500 g) Epsom salt or a combination of Epsom salt and Himalayan salt
- 20 drops relaxing essential oil, such as chamomile, clary sage, lavender, rose, sandalwood, or ylang-ylang
- 2 teaspoons carrier oil (jojoba, sweet almond)
- Dried flower buds, such as lavender if using lavender essential oil, or chamomile, or rose (optional)

1. In a wide-mouth glass jar with a tight-fitting lid, layer the Epsom salt, essential oil, carrier oil, and dried flowers (if using).

2. Cover the jar and shake well to combine the ingredients.

3. Store, tightly sealed, in a cool, dark place.

When the time is right, place some healing crystals that support your needs, and that you have charged by the Sun or Moon's light, around the bath. Pour the contents of the jar into the tub and fill it with warm water. Step in, ease down, and close your eyes. Soak for 20 minutes.

While you feel the comforting softness of the water support you, let the warmth and scent lull you into a space of calm. Thank the hearth goddess for her help and wisdom and find peace in these few moments.

Sweet goddess of the hearth and home whose wisdom I do seek,
Please speak to me of time alone, these tensions to release.
In soothing waters I do hear your whisper, feel your touch.
Your graceful lessons sent my way encourage me to go on.

Step out of the tub, being careful as the oil may make the surface slippery, and wrap yourself in the most luxurious towel you have.

SLEEP RITUALS

Sleep's magical restorative powers help heal body and mind. When sleep eludes, it's often the result of tension, stress, or worries. To help relax the body and mind and invite sleep in, consider these bedtime rituals, or one of your own, to ensure a visit from the Sandman.

A soothing meditation: Maybe after a soothing bath (see page 122), take 10 minutes each night to create a bedtime ritual meditation to calm the mind before climbing under the sheets. About 20 minutes before bedtime, sit quietly in your darkened bedroom, perhaps light a blue candle for its soothing energy (just be sure to extinguish it before bedtime). Breathe quietly, naturally, while keeping your mind clear. If it starts to worry about tomorrow's to-do list, gently bring your attention back to your breathing. Do this for about 10 minutes, or until you feel calmed and able to welcome sweet sleep.

Slumber scents: Diffuse a sleep-friendly essential oil in your bedroom, following the manufacturer's instructions for your diffuser. Along with lavender, rose essential oil has also been shown to help with relaxation, which can lead to better sleep. (If some magical romance is on your mind, the scent of rose can help with that, too!) Add some soothing music for an even greater relaxing sensory experience.

Bedtime journaling: Sometimes those swirling thoughts of the day . . . what went wrong, what was forgotten, what's left for tomorrow, can mean no rest for the weary. Spend 5 to 10 minutes before drifting off to sleep just writing your thoughts from the day—the good, the bad, and the ugly . . . to get them of your mind and help you process any worries. If that's not for you, spend the time making a to-do list for tomorrow so you don't have to keep thinking about it. You may find your mind relieved to be organized and, therefore, more receptive to sleep.

RECIPES FOR HOUSE MAGIC

The ritual of mealtime brings lots of opportunity to stir up some magic in our lives. Add a splash of herbal magic with these simple herb-infused oil and vinegar recipes—no spells required!

Rosemary-Infused Olive Oil

Rosemary typically symbolizes remembrance, but it can also attract romantic love and protection. So, what better potion for creating delicious memories than a dose of rosemary oil. Add a splash to salads or soups, drizzle on pizza, or simply use as a dip for a gorgeous artisan bread. Or, pass a little magic to your friends, when you give this as a gift. Whatever you choose, it will be unforgettable.

- 6 rosemary sprigs, gently washed, dried, and left out overnight to thoroughly dry (water promotes bacterial growth), damaged leaves removed
- 1 cup (240 ml) olive oil, plus more as needed

1. Wash and thoroughly dry two pint-size (480 ml) Mason jars and their lids.
2. Gently bruise or crush the rosemary sprigs to help release their oils.
3. Place the rosemary in one jar, leaving 1 to 2 inches (2.5 to 5 cm) of space at the top.
4. Pour the olive oil over the rosemary, covering the herbs by at least 1 inch (2.5 cm).
5. Cover the jar with a lid and set aside in a cool, dark place for up to 1 week to infuse the oil with the herb's energies and flavor.
6. After three or four days, taste the oil to judge how intense the herbal flavor is. You may want to taste it each day until it develops your desired depth of rosemary flavor.
7. Place a fine-mesh sieve over a clean, dry bowl and strain the oil into it.
8. Discard the rosemary.

9. Transfer the rosemary oil to the second pint-size (480 ml) jar and seal the lid tightly.

10. Keep refrigerated for up to one month. If the oil shows any signs of change or deterioration, such as mold growth, discard immediately and do not use. Bring to room temperature to use.

A dash of oil sprinkles hints of time gone by.
A splash instead delights the head with thoughts of winsome joys.
A dip doth add a heady scent that sings of fond good-byes.
As gift, a sign of future times to cherish by and by.

Basil Balsamic Vinegar

Spice up your mealtime routine with a dash of basil balsamic. This sweet, earthy vinegar is beautifully complemented by the aromatic basil. Basil's magical properties are good for, among other things, fostering family love and boosting luck. For more than just salads, dress grilled meats or vegetables, drizzle over fresh tomatoes and mozzarella or pizza, or dip in a crusty bread or fresh vegetables for a flavor-filled appetizer and a peaceful family meal.

- 1 cup (35 g) packed fresh basil leaves, gently washed and thoroughly dried (water promotes bacterial growth)
- 2 cups (480 ml) balsamic vinegar, plus more as needed (use a good-quality vinegar for best results)

1. Wash and thoroughly dry two 28-ounce (720 ml) Mason jars and their lids.
2. Gently bruise or crush the basil to help release the oils.
3. Place the basil in one jar, leaving 1 to 2 inches (2.5 to 5 cm) of space at the top.
4. Pour the vinegar over the basil, almost filling the jar.
5. Cover the jar with a lid and set aside in a cool, dark place for up to two weeks to infuse the vinegar with the basil's sweet touch.
6. After 3 or 4 days, taste the vinegar to judge how intense the herbal flavor is. You may want to taste it each day until it develops your desired depth of basil flavor.
7. Place a fine-mesh sieve over a clean, dry bowl and strain the vinegar into it.
8. Discard the basil.
9. Transfer the basil balsamic to the second 28-ounce (720 ml) jar and seal the lid tightly.
10. Store in a cool, dark place for up to one year. If the vinegar shows any signs of change or deterioration, such as mold growth, discard immediately and do not use.

If mealtime madness has you in its spell, recast the energy to bring everyone to the table at once!

Sweet basil spin your magic charms, a call to gather 'round
To share the meal presented here, when family time abounds.
No chat, or text, or Instamess . . . it's you I long to see.
So, grab a chair, a fork, a pear!, and tell me how you've been.

SPELLS

Using all you've learned so far, combine color, scent, greenery, light, music, crystals, or other objects that speak to you and make you happy. The tools you need for casting spells are really just a few—set your intentions, trust in yourself, and hold close the desire to do good. Nothing else is required except to choose and use wisely what speaks to you. These charming talismans will focus your mind, invite positive energy, and encourage your hopes and dreams to emanate into the Universe and return home to you in even greater ways.

Majestic they stand,
A journey marked by dreaming,
Mountains and ideals.

SEASONAL SPELLS FOR MANIFESTING INTENTIONS

Just as you would tend a garden according to seasonal changes, tend to your home and life attuned to Nature as well. Use its natural rhythms to adjust your steps and assess progress toward your goals. It matters not how grand or small you wish to change your life. A step or two mastered is progress made in dance as well as life.

WINTER

REST AND REFLECTION

While spending more time within the cozy nest you call home, warmed by its soul and fire, reflect on the best way to care for yourself and your family until you can emerge in the Sun, refreshed and renewed.

When Sun does dip behind the icy curtain of winter's soul,
Our cue, we take, when nights grow long to search within our own.
For time and space do let us see what gladdens and delights,
To set our sails for warmer climes, our target on these sights.

Extinguish flames that burn too bright and blind you from the truth
And set your course upon the star that guides you with its light.

SPRING

INTENTION SETTING

Time for some spring cleaning around the home and hearth, to re-energize your home's happy, healthy vibes. While tidying each room, recite this spell to align your home's spirit with the Universe.

The Earth renews her lively pace and wakens with a smile
As birds and blooms announce their message of rebirth.
I breathe the scents, each element of which imbues the hungry soul
With sweet fresh dreams of wishes new and those yet to behold.

Breathe deeply, in and out, to calm the mind and soul.
Imagine here the growth, so near, your house needs to be whole.

SUMMER

CELEBRATE THE BOUNTY

When summer's call tempts you away from home, remember to nurture your roots, as you'll be back before long.

When summer's chorus calls for us to join its merry song,
We drift and dance and sing and chant the words we've dreamed so long.
For now it's time to reap and feast on plantings we have sown,
To reach our dreams and taste the sweets of that which we have grown.

Rejoice in hopes and dreams and plans and actions you have made.
It's now, my friend, that magic life you've hoped for can be led.

FALL

EVALUATE AND RECOMMIT

If your hobbies include scrapbooking, blogging, photography, or journaling, now is the time to organize your craft corner and record the memories made with friends and family this year.

Congratulate yourself for all the soil hoed
To plant and grow and propagate the life your dreams foretold.
But time it is to set aside the tools that served you well
And take great stock of what you have and what still needs to grow.

Rest, relax, and celebrate the goals reached by this day,
But ask your heart what happens next and heed its chosen spell.

ROUND ROBIN WISHES

As the cheerful robin now resides year-round in many places, the odds of your home and family being touched by her good luck charms are greatly improved. Open a window and let the robin's uplifting voice sing backup to life's celebrations, which often include a wish—over a lost tooth, birthday candles, a shooting star, or for something bigger like finding a new home or true love. No matter the object of your lucky desires, let Mrs. Robin lend a hand.

Chirp, trill, burble, tweet—
What cheerful song you sing,
For though not Irish of descent,
The luck you bring is sweet.
So, chirp, trill, burble, tweet from sunrise to sunset . . .
Each lovely note a penny dropped into my wishing well.

PEACE

Whether keeping the peace among siblings, between partners, or in that fine line between work life and home life, Nature soothes. When seeking literal peace and quiet in the home, or peace for the mind and soul, her sights, sensations, colors, and sounds can ground you when needed most.

Wind whispers, rain cries, blossoms laugh, Sun warms.
Leaves chatter, snow calms, grass beckons, trees wave.
Moon soothes, Earth grows, stars light, planets play.
Pick a time, just once each day, when peace and quiet reign.

LIVE, LAUGH, LOVE, DREAM, RENEW
HOME

HOUSE MAGIC

The shelter your home provides gives you so many things: warmth, protection, peace, and pride, to name a few. To live in the moment means not taking anything for granted. Appreciate the bounty your home nurtures.

You've worked so hard to bring your home in line with your desires.
Aware you'll be when energies do shift and cause a mire.
Investigate the space in which you feel the ebb and flow.
Adjust you can, with spells at hand, to tend the hearth's warm fires.

PROTECTING THE HOME FROM ILLNESS AND HARM

Look to the Full Moon to offer her most protective charms when searching for ways to keep your home safe from health issues—both physical and mental. Seek her brightly shining healing light. Cast this spell in rooms throughout the home where people gather, to keep them healthy and happy.

Full Moon, with your great power
Reach down and pull the grief and ills from this hour.
Keep us safe while isolated
In our silent ivory towers.

ENTRYWAY

It is believed by the Irish that upon entering a new home, *you must also leave through the same door* to ensure luck flows into the home . . . except at the witching hour on New Year's Eve, when in the front and out the back you must go to sweep in a lucky new year.

Set the tone for your home and life with a welcome mat or sign so that all feel love who enter here.

This home abounds with life and love and welcomes all who come.
For multiplied these joys do thrive when shared by more than one.
The love and laughter echo on and, yes, the house does smile.

EXIT

Sometimes being happy and productive means giving something up—things that no longer bring us joy just hold us back. Take a quiet moment to listen to your heart. It will tell you what no longer belongs to you and needs to be relinquished.

An exit is not a journey's end; it marks a spot in time
Where once I stood and faced the Sun, but now the Sun's declined.
So, turn and face the other way to seek the door I need
To lead me to another spot to plant, to grow—succeed.

BID EVIL SPIRITS AND GERMS ADIEU

Doors and windows are prime entry spots for evil to lurk. Keep entryways and windows clean and clear, sprinkle a little Himalayan salt nearby, and let sit for twenty-four hours to absorb negative energies, then sweep or vacuum any potential harm away. This short chant can't hurt either.

This home is blessed by light of day and charmed by dark of night.
Where love abounds no evil is found nor harmful agents be.
With grains of salt and besom broom, I cast you from this site.

NEW TRADITIONS

Whether a new home, New Year, new family member, or new job, the reasons to celebrate new traditions in our lives, and temper the fear of change are countless. Living a loving life based in the present moment gives us something new to celebrate in our home each day. A simple spell of intention to recognize opportunities is all you need to begin.

New day, new path, new hopes, new dreams;
The new soon will feel old.
Each day, each path, each hope, each dream,
Holds countless tales untold.
With open heart and mind I pray
To journey forth renewed
With strength and joy along the way—as old turns into new.

KEEP SAFE AND SECURE

Physical, emotional, and spiritual safety are our rights in our homes. Let nothing threaten them—ever.

Let lock and key deter those who might intend me harm.
Let spirit guide who dwells inside protect this house with charm.
With earthly strength and heaven's might, I shroud myself in courage
That unseen dragons lying wait do slink away discouraged.

UNWANTED PESTS

Be they mice under the stairs, birds eating your newly planted garden seeds, squirrels, deer, raccoons, skunks, or any other pests, like weeds, are really just animals in the wrong places. No need to do them harm, but do set down the law—and a hefty border of citrus peels, cayenne pepper, cinnamon, and other natural repellents.

O' Mr. Skunk and Ms. Whitetail, and all your other friends, please hear this day, your lease to stay is hereby at an end. So, pack your things—be gone, I say, I bid you fair adieu.

KEEPING EVERYDAY ILLNESS AND VIRUSES AWAY

Keeping ourselves and our family well is important to keeping the home running smoothly and with good energy vibes. Add a touch of protective energy from the Universe to keep illness and viruses away from your home and loved ones. Tuck a clear quartz crystal (see page 108), the master healer, under your pillow, or turquoise (see page 113) for its overall healing powers.

Before that under-the-weather feeling hits, take a moment to actively protect your home.

I bid you, illness, melt away and leave this house unharmed.
I pray for rest to heal what's left that life resets its norms.

CELEBRATE, HOPE, GROW, GATHER
LIVING ROOM

HOSPITALITY

Though no longer the scarce luxury or symbol of wealth and status, the pineapple is a traditional sign of welcome. Whether adorning a sumptuous feast or signaling the sea captain's safe return home, this luscious fruit is always a treat. So, whether fresh fruit or tea, flowers or sweet soaps, those extra-special things you do to welcome people and make them feel at home are always appreciated.

Hello, my friend, please do step in, and welcome to my home.
You've journeyed far and long and wide, and safely have arrived.
We celebrate and raise a glass, so glad that you have come!

WELCOMING NEW FRIENDS

New friendships expand our souls and our homes. When new friendships blossom, a simple welcoming spell can set the energies in motion. Sit quietly in the room where friends and family gather most, such as a den, living room, or playroom. Wear or hold clear quartz or rose quartz to enhance the friendly vibrations, or garnet to help send your inviting message into the world to be received by others. Imagine:

Friends. Gather. Home. Filled.
Hearts. Matter. Cares. Stilled.
Love. Nurture. Lives. Build.

GATHERING

Gather all those new friends you've made and introduce them to the clan.

When gathered here, it's "thanks" I say to Goddess of the Realm,
For tending dear the fires here that keep the family warm.
With old and new around the hearth, it's time to toast the cheer
That brightens and encircles all among us here.

LOSS

Loss comes in all forms in families. When you've experienced a simple loss that just has you a bit out of sorts, take a moment to consider all you do have to be grateful for. Write it down if it helps the thoughts stick.

If you need a hug from the Universe and a little self-love to get you back in action, sprinkle a few drops of rose essential oil on a pink or white candle. Light the candle on a heatproof surface and gaze into the flame, letting it and the oil's scent relax you. When you're ready, invite your favorite domestic goddess, the Earth, Sun, or Moon, to sit with you.

I light this candle to remind myself that darkness can turn bright.
I light this candle to dispel the stormy mood I fight, for loss and doubt have turned my will into a frozen plight.
I seek the candle's warmth to thaw the cold that's gripped my heart, its glow to find that piece of me that's ready to restart.

PATIENCE

Kids underfoot? New to home schooling? How's that DIY going? Laundry room look like a rummage sale? Water heater leaking? With life comes the opportunity for our patience to be tried and tested. When those times confront you, a simple spell can help refocus your thoughts on the positive and get back to the task at hand.

Visualize the color blue: the wide-open sky, the ocean on a sunny day, your favorite blue flowers, or any swath of blue. Take a deep breath, in and out, breathing in the calming color and breathing out the tenseness of stress.

Each breath in restores calm. It fills me head to toe.
Each breath out creates space, releasing any woes.
When storm clouds clear, the sky appears much bluer than before.

CONNECTION, MEMORY, ABUNDANCE, TOGETHERNESS

FAMILY ROOM

JOY TO YOUR WORLD

Like the beauty of a magnificent sunset and the joy it brings, crystals in the orange color family vibrate with joy. One of the best crystals for promoting positive energy and happiness is citrine, with its sunny yellow color. Place a crystal in the family room to promote a positive vibe, or wear or carry one with you. Be sure to charge or transfer your intentions to the crystal before placing it. Repeat the following three times:

Joy beams from my heart each day.

FAMILY CONNECTIONS

If family holds an important place in your life plan and the family room is the place you connect most, decorate the space with meaningful objects that reflect each family member and consider a simple visualization to absorb the energies from this room and carry them with you each day to tap into when life gets crazy.

Take a few minutes to sit comfortably and quietly in the room, close your eyes, and visualize memories made here that make you happy.

It's in this room my spirits soar when gathered all as one.
Each one of you contributes to the richness of my life and
Gives each day, in countless ways, more brightness than the Sun.

ANIMAL COMPANIONS

New animal in your home? Here's some help to inspire the perfect name for your new family member. Hold the wiggly bundle in your arms and feel the warmth and energy meld with yours. Let it fill you with wonder that such a small creature can offer such immense love and trust.

Your eyes so bright, with love and hope they shine. Your ears and tail do shim and shake—not to mention your behind!

A name you need by which to heed the call from all your fans—a name befitting royalty, for soon you'll be the star.

Of neighborhood and play dates, too, and backyard jamborees . . . I have the perfect name in mind, which I bestow on you.

SUPPORT

Sometimes family meetings can be a way to clear the air, or reset the course and establish expectations. While not everyone looks forward to these, take the opportunity to clear the negative energy and fill the space with positive emotions.

Consider diffusing an essential oil, such as sweet orange, lemon, or peppermint, which are all good for clearing the negative and promoting the positive. Take a moment to sit quietly before the gathering, breathing in the healing scents, if using.

Though sailing is not smooth right now, the winds will soon abate.
With calmer seas and clearer skies, the course we can correct.
With truth and love and honesty, our family will connect.

GAME NIGHT

Gather 'round with friends and family to show a little friendly competition—not for who can win, but for who can have the most fun. A laughter-filled home radiates love.

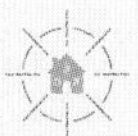

Take a seat. Ante up. Invoke your lucky charm.
For who remains at end of game inherits the whole farm.
And with it comes the right to brag—but first, you must prevail.
For I do cast this spell that fun remains the moral of this tale.

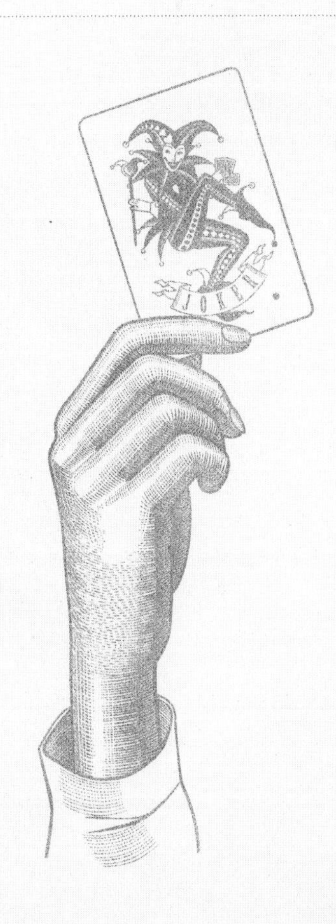

HEAL, CLEAN, RESTORE
BATHROOM

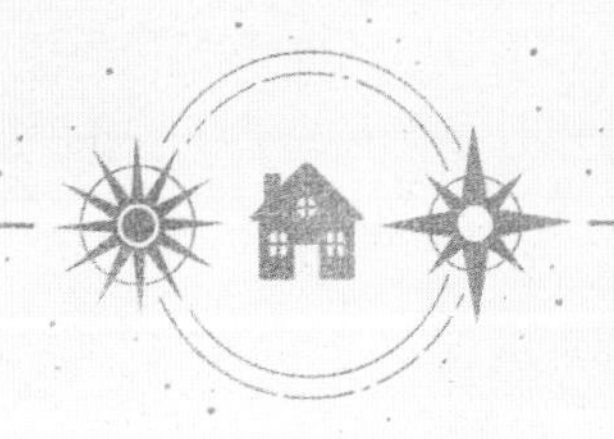

SOOTHING BOO-BOOS

Life's little boo-boos can knock us all out of whack. Use the bath's healing waters to gently clean the wound and apply a magical bandage from the medicine cabinet. With a few words, the healing will begin.

I saved this magic bandage. It's been waiting just for you.
To wrap your tender boo-boo, to gently heal and soothe.
I kiss your magic bandage—now, you'll soon be good as new!

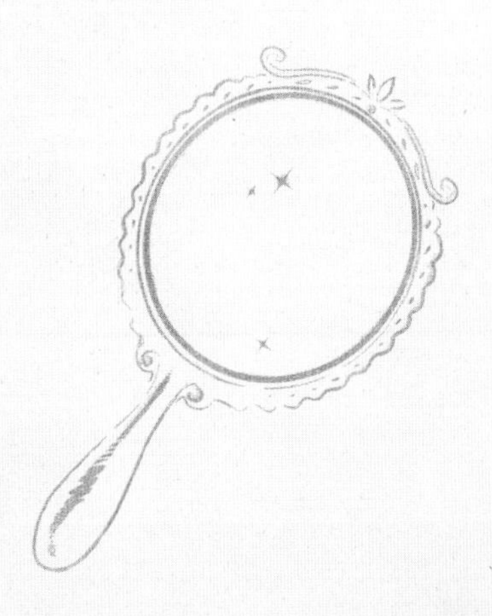

SUGAR SCRUB FOR SWEET LOVE

Whether you prefer a sweet-smelling lotion or homemade sugar scrub, draw some attention your way. Liberally apply the potion and watch the bees swarm—with a little boost from this spell.

Sweet scent awake the sense of love about to bloom.
Sweet nectar flow from head to toe. Its honey, sweet perfume.
Sweet love release your fragrant joy and luscious tempting tune.

HAPPY HANDS

Whether to cleanse yourself from the day's work, or protect yourself from unseen viruses and germs, washing your hands should be a frequent occurrence in this room. Teach little ones proper technique and remind big ones not to hurry. You know the tune . . . let's get washin'!

Lather up well with soap.
For those germs, there's no hope!

Rinse it all down the drain away . . . keeping healthy is no joke!

Lather. Rinse. Repeat.

FOCUS, CLARITY, CREATIVITY, EASE
OFFICE

PROSPERITY

Boost home office vibes with a money plant. According to feng shui, a plant with rounded leaves, such as a jade plant, is bound to bring luck and prosperity. Adorn your desk or a shelf with crystals as well, and set a focused, creative, prosperous atmosphere. Consider citrine, jade, or tiger's eye. An incantation as you place the items will set their energies in motion.

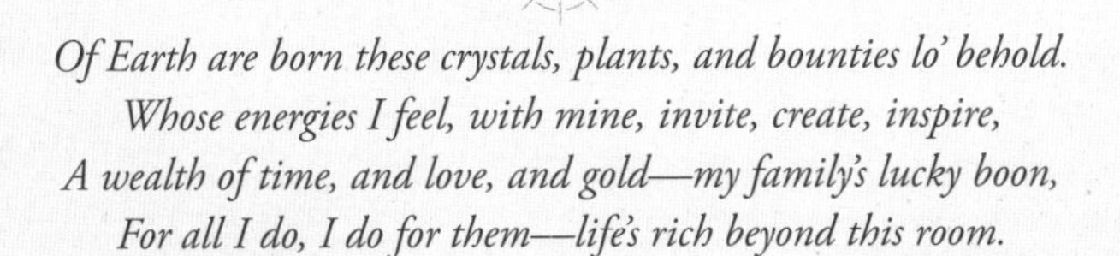

Of Earth are born these crystals, plants, and bounties lo' behold.
Whose energies I feel, with mine, invite, create, inspire,
A wealth of time, and love, and gold—my family's lucky boon,
For all I do, I do for them—life's rich beyond this room.

CREATIVITY

Orange is said to be the color of creativity; it is born of the attraction of red's energy and fire to yellow's happiness. When creativity eludes and that deadline nears, surround yourself with orange, close your eyes, and visualize its creative vibrations flowing throughout your body. Try this affirmation to heighten your belief in your innate abilities:

I am fire. I am joy. When wed, they create anew.
Inventive glow within my soul is nourished by your hue.

SUCCESS

Thyme, spearmint, and basil are known to attract wealth and success, as does the color green. Consider adding a few plants to your workspace, or diffusing their essential oils, if you are able.

It's time, dear thyme, for luck to bloom—I feel the energy.
And basil smells of sweet success, like money from a tree.
O' lovely mint, whose whispered charms are music to my ears,
Your soft refrain, repeated thrice, tells of my newfound fame.

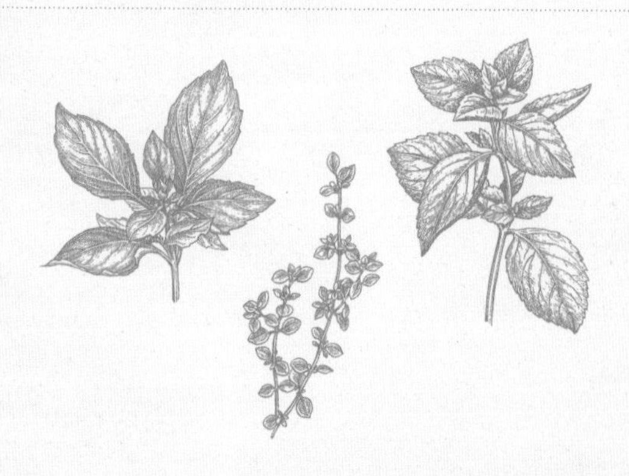

LESS THAN SUCCESS

For those times when things at the office feel stalled or look like less than your planned achievements, gaze upon the Waning Gibbous Moon, the perfect time to stop and reflect on the best way forward on the path to success. Progress is measured in steps forward but can only be appreciated by a look back.

I've worked so hard and progress made brings pride—a hearty cheer!
But time grows old and so, I'm told, do I just sitting here.
I see the wrinkle in the plan—the speed bump was the clue.
I'll not be slowed or swayed or cowed—I dust off and resume.

NOURISHMENT, GRATITUDE, ENERGY

KITCHEN AND DINING AREAS

PRESERVE THIS HOME

In the same way you can use your kitchen to preserve the culinary magic of fresh herbs, use the magical properties of the herbs to help preserve your home. Keep it safe from negative energies, illness, strife, and bad luck.

Blend your fresh, finely chopped herbs of choice (see page 72) with a bit of olive oil to form a paste. Freeze the paste in ice cube trays. Once solid, transfer to an airtight freezer bag and keep frozen for up to six months. Toss into sauces, soups, and stews with a simple nod to their benefits:

Preserve—protect, defend from harm; these herbs I hold, still safe and bold, do so enhance my soup!
Preserve—protect, defend from harm; your herbal scent, its magic meant to shield from unseen threat.

SHARING IS CARING

Let the magic of meals conjured in your kitchen spread love and sustenance beyond the walls of your home. Invite others to join you around the table or take meals to those unable to leave their homes. When we can share our good fortune (no matter the wealth), our bounty grows threefold.

With mindful heart I honor Earth. Her bounty never ends.
And blessed be, we share this meal with family and with friends.
The foods we eat, the wine we share, clean water that we have,
Are gifts bestowed, for much we owe, which multiply when shared.

MORNING, SUNSHINE

Say this spell before you take the first sip of water or coffee in the morning:

For water and for coffee, thank you, Earth, for gifts these two.
As once combined, their magic shines within this robust brew.
First cup in hand I toast the day—I'll face it after two!

WATER

In our homes we nourish with it, cleanse with it, play with it, grow with it, quench thirst with it, and can take its easy access for granted. Each time you throw in that laundry, fill a teakettle, draw a bath, or turn on a sprinkler, offer up a silent prayer for water's gifts. Life.

One hydrogen, two oxygens—miraculous. Water.
So everywhere, so everyday, I hardly give a blink.
Our life depends so much on you, we must preserve, protect,
And gratefully acknowledge each renewing drop we drink.

CAULDRON OF NOURISHMENT

Your kitchen serves as command central for nourishing yourself and your family. Nourishing their spirits and souls can be a bit daunting—with needs so vast indeed, each one uniquely true. Reach for your trusty cauldron to concoct this blessed stew. While no real recipe exists, add what you have, call on your kitchen spirits for what you need, and your family will be sustained no end.

A dash of basil for great courage when rocky roads prevail.
A frond of dill, a sprig of mint—keep safe along life's trail.
A pinch of sage for in those times when wisdom it does fail,
And yarrow leaves to heal what hurts and comfort what does ail.
Some cinnamon, when sprinkled on, smells sweetly of success,
With lavender and chamomile for sleep and peaceful rest.
So, stir and sip and add a dash of salt for flavor's sake—
My wish for you, a seasoned life, is there for you to take.

REST, REFLECTION, ROMANCE, PEACE
BEDROOM

NEW MOON, NEW ROMANCE

If your bedroom is seeing a little too much sleep and not quite enough romance, take a moment to search your heart for what's really important in a romantic partner. Gather a small bouquet: fern for magic; ivy for fidelity; red rose for passion. Set your intentions accordingly. Invite the New Moon to sit and reflect on the chance for new beginnings. If the Moon sees into your true and good heart, her guidance is given freely.

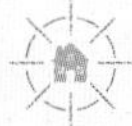

New love I seek to fill my heart, my home, my life.
A love that sparks, and grows, and lasts through good times and the strife.
A love that honors you and me, a love with passion burns,
I seek, dear Moon, your growing light, my lover's face upturn.

SLEEPY-TIME SPELL

After indulging in a sleep ritual (see page 126), a little spell to enhance your good work won't hurt. Or soothe a restless child with these comforting words to quietly re-enter dreamland. Lie quietly and comfortably in bed and reflect:

I listen for the quiet now. It fills my ears—an emptiness of space and sound.
I fill the space with peace and calm, relaxing breath to ease the stress.
My mind, it drifts, and that's okay, as gentle sleep comes near to stay.

SOOTHING SLEEP

Calming an overactive mind that won't let you sleep, can be as simple as counting your blessings.

Greet each sunrise with celebration and gratitude anew
For time should not be wasted now, or set aside to stew.
So, feel the blossoms in your heart grow larger with each breath,
And scatter they to mark the way along the path you choose.
Rejoice and pray to thank the day—each minute is a gift.

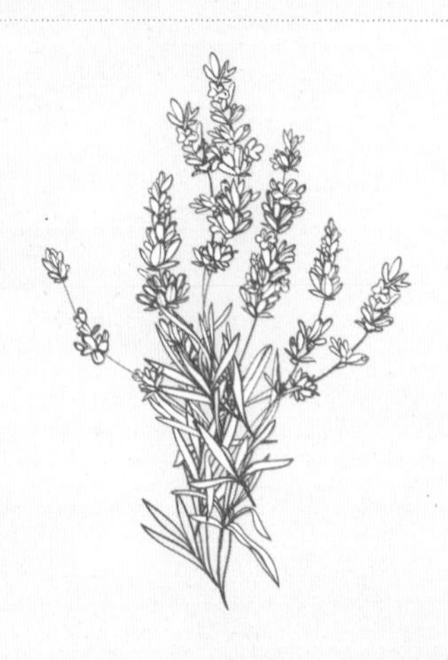

DREAMS

Tuck a sprig of hyacinth, lavender, or thyme under your pillow before bedtime to induce sweet dreams. Lie comfortably and visualize the dream you would like to visit you tonight. As you drift off to sleep, repeat:

With magic herbs to scent my dreams, what stories they will tell.
Of meadows free and shining seas and wonders to behold.
The Moon bestows a gentle kiss and whispers in my ear,
"Sweet dreams tonight. Rest well. Sleep tight.
New day dawns bright and clear."

SOOTHING A FRIGHTENED CHILD

When monsters creep into sweet dreams or otherwise scare from places dark and deep, there is no time to waste. Those wrenching tears and fears must go—right along with the monsters. You can use a plain water spray or a calming essential oil spray, such as lavender, to restore soothing order for restful sleep.

Turn on the lights, make a quick sweep of the room for evidence, and spray the anti-monster remedy anywhere it's needed. These soothing words will encourage the child to sleep and the monster to retreat:

Let's wipe the tears and calm the fears with hugs—and kisses, too.
Those monsters only want to play—they do not mean to scare.
Say, "Monster, go! Don't tarry so, for sleep is on the way."

Now gentle one, do snuggle up and close your lovely eyes.
With Sandman's tune, you're soon a-snooze, as monsters wave bye-bye.

TRUE LOVE

If things feel a little lackluster in the romance department and it's what's missing from a fully magical life, open your heart and mind to the many possibilities around you. Turn to your crystals for a little energy nudge to get things flowing. Consider stashing them by your bedside, under your pillow, or on an altar set up in your bedroom dedicated to love and romance. Choose:

- **Amethyst** soothes conflict, if that's what's in your way.
- **Blue lace agate** speaks from the heart, for honest communication and building trust to establish a new, or rebuild anew, relationship.
- **Garnet** stimulates passion, communicates your desires to your intended, and inspires sweep-me-off-my-feet romance.
- **Malachite** helps heal past hurts and opens your heart and mind to accept love again.
- **Rose quartz** reminds you to love yourself first; others will love you in return.

Remember to clear your crystals before working with them, set your intentions, and offer thanks for their help.

I choose these crystals for their brightly burning loving charms—
Bid amour return and passion burn, to hold within my arms.
And light the fire within my eyes that say, "Yes, look my way,"
When sparks do fly and fears do die—romance will seize the day.

NEW BABY

Children light the home with their innocent magic in ways unanticipated. If you're thinking of growing your family, lean on this secret spell to cast a fertile wish.

It's hard to know just when the time is right for what I seek:
A tiny little you or me—my longing's at a peak.
Sweet stars and Moon, and Earth below, please listen to my prayer,
Please bless me with your fertile luck, this gift I wish to bear.

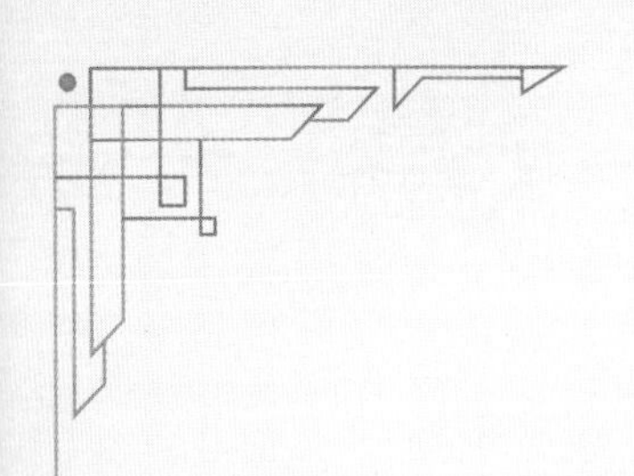
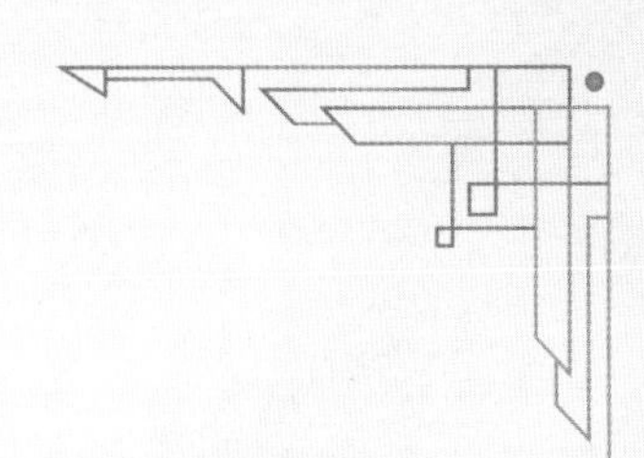

Here within, I hope you've felt the wisdom of a friend,

To lend an ear, to hold a hand, to travel to the end.

With tales, and tips, and spells to brew sweet magical delight

You're charged to carry on the work to bring each day to life.

Be kind to Earth, her feelings are not always given heed.

By tending them, we guarantee a blooming world indeed.

And so you've learned along the way, a "house" is just four walls

But making it a "home," I say, needs love most above all.

Blessed be.

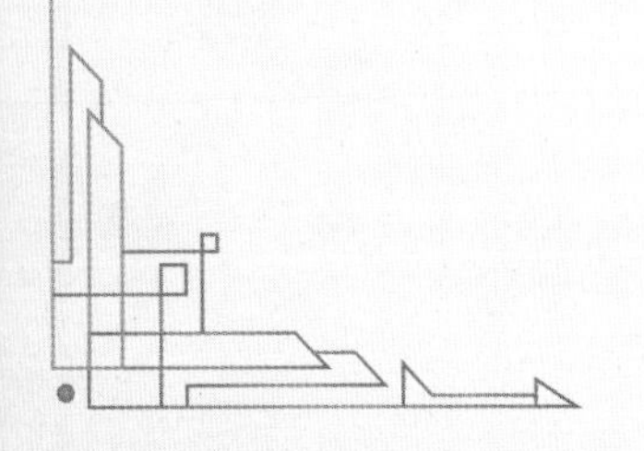
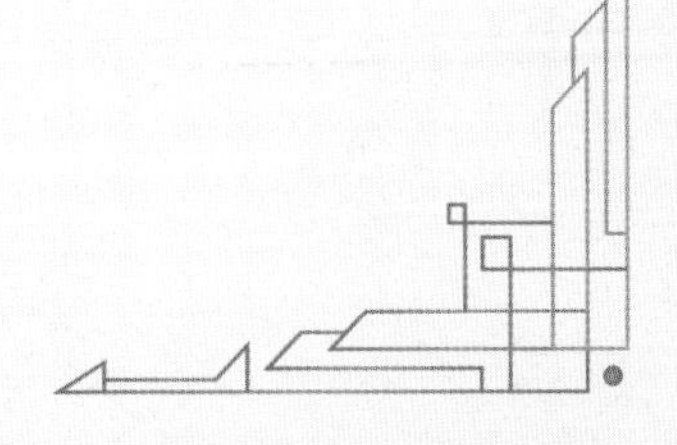

Resources and References

Ancient History Encyclopedia: Ancient.eu

Ancient Origins: ancient-origins.net

Bob Vila: Bobvila.com

Crystal Dictionary: CystalDictionary.com

Crystalinks: Crystalinks.com

Encyclopaedia Britannica: Britannica.com

Energy Muse: energymuse.com

Ferguson, Yuna L., and Kennon M. Sheldon, "Trying to Be Happier Really Can Work: Two Experimental Studies." The Journal of Positive Psychology 8, no. 1 (2013): 23–33. https://doi.org/10.1080/17439760.2012.747000

Gem Select: GemSelect.com

Gemological Institute of America: GIA.edu

Good Housekeeping: GoodHousekeeping.com

Greenaway, Kate. *Language of Flowers*. The Project Gutenberg eBook. www.gutenberg.org. http://www.gutenberg.org/3/1/5/9/31591

Himalayan Salt Company: HimalayanSaltusa.com

House Beautiful: HouseBeautiful.com

International Gem Society: GemSociety.org

Kitchn: thekitchn.com

Mountain Rose Herbs: www.mountainrose herbs.com

Mythical Ireland: MythicalIreland.com

National Aeronautics and Space Administration: nasa.gov

National Association for Holistic Aromatherapy: naha.org

Paciorek, Andrew L. Strange Lands: *Supernatural Creatures of the Celtic Otherworld.* www.batcow.co.uk/strangelands/domestic.htm

Psychology Today: PsychologyToday.com

Smithsonian: Smithsonianmag.com

Smithsonian Learning Lab: LearningLab.si.edu

Soul & Spirit: SoulandSpiritMagazine.com

Tarot: Tarot.com

The Harvard Gazette: news.harvard.edu

The Metropolitan Museum of Art: MetMuseum.org

The Old Farmer's Almanac: www.almanac.com

The Witchipedia: Witchipedia.com

WebMD: WebMD.com

Wigington, Patti. "Earth Folklore and Legends." Learn Religions. Accessed January 29, 2020. learnreligions.com/earth-element-folklore-and-legends-2561685

Yoga Journal: YogaJournal.com

INDEX

Acknowledgments

I am most gratefully indebted to Rage Kindelsperger for her trust and creative leadership. This second magical book lives because of her. Words of kindness sprinkle like raindrops to renew.

Thank you to Keyla Pizarro-Hernández for her steady hand and kind heart. Books are born of collaboration, and I'm glad you're on my team.

To my sister, Gaye, for always knowing what to say when life is not so magical.

Finally, to my love, John, whose very presence in my life is proof magic exists.